Richard III and the Bosworth Campaign

To all who fought at Bosworth Field,
on whichever side they fought

Richard III and the Bosworth Campaign

Revised Paperback Edition

Peter Hammond

Pen & Sword
MILITARY

First published in Great Britain in 2010
Revised paperback edition 2013
by Pen & Sword Military
an imprint of
Pen & Sword Books Ltd
47 Church Street
Barnsley
South Yorkshire
S70 2AS

ISBN 978 1 78337 616 2

Typeset in 11pt Ehrhardt by
Mac Style, Bridlington, E. Yorkshire

Printed and bound in the UK by CPI Group (UK) Ltd, Croydon,
CRO 4YY

Pen & Sword Books Ltd incorporates the imprints of Pen & Sword
Archaeology, Atlas, Aviation, Battleground, Discovery, Family History,
History, Maritime, Military, Naval, Politics, Railways, Select, Social
History, Transport, True Crime, and Claymore Press, Frontline Books,
Leo Cooper, Praetorian Press, Remember When, Seaforth Publishing
and Wharncliffe.

For a complete list of Pen & Sword titles please contact
PEN & SWORD BOOKS LIMITED
47 Church Street, Barnsley, South Yorkshire, S70 2AS, England
E-mail: enquiries@pen-and-sword.co.uk
Website: www.pen-and-sword.co.uk

Contents

Acknowledgements

I would like to thank Richard Knox and Richard Mackinder for talking over their work on the battlefield and showing us round the splendid new Bosworth Battlefield Centre. Thanks are also due to the organisers and the speakers at the splendid conference on 20 February 2010 in Leicester when the results of the archaeological survey work and the new site for the battle were finally revealed, which gave me much to think about. I would also like to thank Lesley Boatwright for patiently translating Latin phrases for me when they did not make a lot of sense (to me), Cris Reay for sharing with me her thoughts on where the battle may have been fought and Frederick Hepburn for the information about the so-called Henry VII wedding medallion and for discussing it with me. It is also important to thank Geoffrey Wheeler for drawing the maps and for supplying very many of the illustrations from his immense collection. I would finally like to thank Carolyn my wife, for patiently listening to my ideas on Bosworth for what may have seemed a very long time, for reading the text of the book and commenting about it with her usual good sense.

List of Illustrations

York and Lancaster

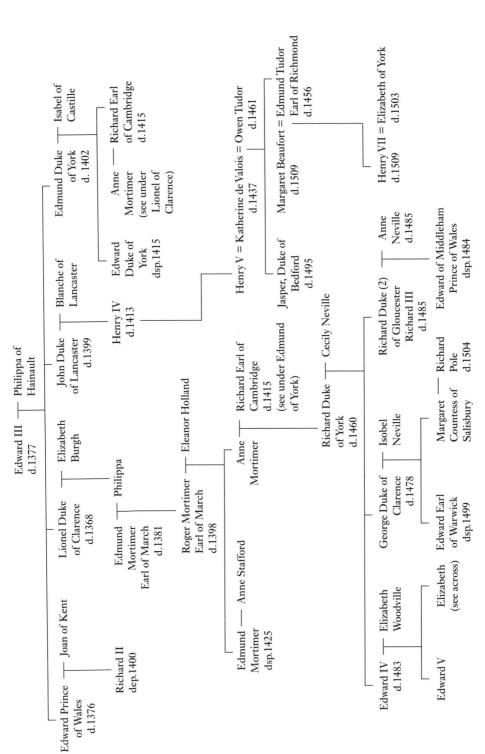

Preface

The battle of Bosworth was traditionally said to mark the end of the Middle Ages, and in at least one sense it did. It is of major importance in English history. A crowned and anointed king died there, the last king of the Plantagenet dynasty that had ruled England since 1154, to be succeeded by the first king of a new dynasty. In addition, it marked, if not the end of the Wars of the Roses, then the last throes of the struggles of the last 30 years, although contemporaries did not know that. Certainly after Bosworth the world changed radically.

In contrast to most battles in the Middle Ages, the battle of Bosworth is relatively well documented. There are several sources – one of which, Polydore Vergil's *History*, is very detailed – which give us information about the course of the battle, although none of the sources is very clear on exactly where it took place and until recently many different places near its probable site near Sutton Cheney in Leicestershire have been proposed. Some of the early sources, notably Edward Hall in his *Chronicle* and William Burton in his *Description of Leicestershire* (1622), place it correctly on a plain. The most popular site, however, has been on and around Ambion Hill, a place first mentioned by Holinshed as the place on which Richard camped, and subsequently taken up enthusiastically by most seventeenth-century and later descriptions as the place where the battle was fought, particularly in William Hutton's popular book *The Battle of Bosworth Field* (2nd edn, 1812). While taking up a defensive position on top of a hill was not unknown in the Middle Ages, there is no evidence that this battle was fought from a hill. None of the contemporary sources says this, nor indeed the later ones, but most writers from the late seventeenth century until recently have placed the battle somewhere near the hill in more or less likely places for a battle, and with equally puzzling maps. In 1990 Peter Foss examined the local evidence in conjunction with the documents and placed the battle on the plain between Ambion Hill, Dadlington, Shenton and Stoke Golding, although even Foss placed Richard's army at the foot of the hill. He also found a place called Sandford, the name of the place at which Richard was probably killed. Foss's site recommended itself to historians until Michael Jones, writing in 2002, suggested that it was fought about 2 miles northeast of Merevale Abbey.

There is a small amount of circumstantial evidence for this suggestion, chiefly in the form of local place-names, such as King Dick's Hole, Bloody Bank and Royal Meadow, that might show that it was fought here but none of the names can be shown to date back as far as the fifteenth century and there is nothing definite to prove that this was the site of the battle. Henry certainly spent the night before Bosworth at Merevale Abbey, but that does not mean that the battle was fought near there. Pinpointing the actual site of the battle has taken a great deal of work in the area around the possible battlefield site, using modern scientific techniques and old-fashioned site-walking to track down the place where this important battle was fought. The results of this work seem to show that the battle took place on a fairly restricted site rather to the south and west of the others suggested. However, the results of the recent work are to some extent preliminary, and it may be that future results will give us a different picture and the battle will be found to have been fought on a slightly different site. Given the current results, it is unlikely to be in a totally different place. However, bearing this in mind (and the fact that future discoveries may change the picture somewhat), this account is based on the results to date.

In addition to not knowing until recently where the battle was actually fought, it has also had several names since 1485. The earliest record we have calls it Redemore or Redesmore. This is an entry in the minutes of the York City Council (the House Books), probably on 23 August. It is written at the end of an entry for 19 August on one folio and before the entry recording the death of Richard III at the top of the next folio, which is dated 23 August and where it is also called Redemore. This news came from John Spooner, who may well have been at the battle. The entry in the House Books on 24 August says that Henry was proclaimed and crowned at the field of Redemore.[1] It is also called Redesmore in notes written in London in 1485/1486.[2] The name Redemoor (or Redmoor) derives from a reedy and perhaps marshy area in the parishes of Dadlington and Shenton. However, the proclamation by Henry VII announcing his accession, entered in the York House Books on 25 August, calls it Sandeford. As mentioned above, Peter Foss has found a possible site for Sandford, and the new work has not yet found another.[3] It has in fact been argued, by Tim Thornton, that the name is not really topographical at all but derives from the works of Thomas the Rymer of Erceldoune.[4] The first record of the name Bosworth for the battle, taken from Market Bosworth, the nearest large settlement, first appears in the Great Chronicle of London, written about 1512, and this was followed by other, later, London chronicles. This name is the one used almost universally since, although a royal document of 1511 does refer to 'Bosworth Field, otherwise called Dadlington Field'.[5]

This book is about the events leading up to this important battle and gives a description of the battle itself. It is also an account of the reign of Richard III, although it is not purely biographical. It concentrates on the military aspects of the two years he held the crown, describing how he fought to ensure the safety of his realm and prevent invasion, and indeed to hold on to his crown. Following the events of Richard's life from his coronation to his death, it is very apparent that from the beginning of his reign he was determined to maintain his position, which is of course what we would expect of any medieval king, but in the case of Richard III it does appear that his kingship had something of the nature of a crusade. He seems to have felt that he was responsible not only for the governance of the realm but for its moral well-being too. It has been suggested that he saw himself as having a moral duty and right to take the throne, perhaps because of the doubts cast on his brother's marriage, as a result of which Edward V (his brother's son) had no moral right to the throne, and that as a man of deep religious convictions, he persuaded himself – or allowed himself to be persuaded – that taking the throne was the right thing to do.[6] Such a man would believe that for him to hold the crown was a God-given right. Richard's various proclamations, particularly that against Tudor in 1485, are couched in very moralistic terms. It is also very apparent that he took every possible practical step to counter the threat of invasion and to meet it when it came. His actions were almost text-book in their thoroughness to raise men and to ensure that he could gather an army as quickly as possible. He always thought and acted as a soldier. At no point in his reign did he seem to have given way to inertia or despair, he responded to all the challenges arising and he fought, literally, to the very end.

Prologue

On 9 April 1483 Edward IV died, possibly from a stroke. He had lingered on after a first stroke about ten days earlier and premature news of his death had arrived in York on 6 April (or possibly 11 April[1]) and the Dean of York ordered a requiem mass to be held. Edward was buried in Windsor on 19 April and was succeeded by his young son Edward, Prince of Wales, who was proclaimed king as Edward V. The prince was in Ludlow on the marches of Wales, where he was being brought up, and heard the news there on 14 April. Edward succeeded peaceably enough, although there was underlying tension between the Woodvilles, the family of the queen, and the new king's paternal relations in the person of the Duke of Gloucester, the only surviving brother of Edward IV, and his supporters. Even before the funeral of Edward IV there had been discussions in the council as to how many men should be in the escort of the young king. One party wished to limit the numbers, obviously for fear of an overwhelming force arriving in London, and believing that such a force would entrench the influence of the queen's relations in the life of the new king. Lord Hastings, Chamberlain to the late king, threatened to retire to his lieutenancy of Calais (a clear threat since the garrison at Calais was England's only large standing force of armed men) if a moderate-sized escort was not agreed. Edward's officers and council in Ludlow had been very much in the hands of allies of the Woodvilles, the queen's family, and his Governor had been his uncle Lord Rivers, the queen's eldest brother. The queen proposed that the escort for the new king should be 2,000 men and this was agreed, although it was obviously a formidable force. Further discussion in the council was about ruling the country while the king was a minor, as he was only a few months over

12 years of age and would need to have a guardian until he was old enough to rule for himself. The council had already agreed that he should be crowned on Sunday, 4 May, as soon as possible in fact. The council also decided that the young king should be governed by a council with the Duke of Gloucester as chief member, and not by a Protector in the person of the duke. The queen's party feared Gloucester might wish to exact retribution for their part in the death of his brother the Duke of Clarence, or indeed might usurp the throne, and wanted to keep him under some control. The decision to have an early coronation would have meant that any protectorate would be very short-lived in any case because these roles traditionally ended after a young king was crowned.[2]

The Duke of Gloucester was in the north, probably at his castle of Middleham in North Yorkshire, and according to Mancini heard the news by messenger from Lord Hastings. Gloucester apparently left Middleham for London, via York, as soon as he possibly could, arriving in York on or before 24 April. Here another requiem mass for the late king was held and all the leading men of the area swore an oath of fealty to the new king, the duke himself taking the oath first. He had already written to the queen and council assuring them of his loyalty to Edward V and asking only that his just deserts as the king's only paternal uncle be recognised, a reference to his claim to be Protector.[3] The York city council took advantage of the duke's presence to agree to send with him John Brackenbury, the mayor's esquire of the mace, to ask him to intercede with the new king for a reduction in the amount of tax they paid. As king, Richard afterwards granted them this (see below), and in fact, despite his worries and the press of other affairs, he took time to write to the York council on 5 June to assure them that he had not forgotten them, sending the letter by John Brackenbury. The duke took advantage of his visit to York to borrow money to help with his expenses, from (among others) Miles Metcalfe, the City's Recorder and one of the duke's council.[4]

The duke must have left York almost immediately, as he was approaching Nottingham by 26 April. Moving on, by 29 April he was in Northampton, where he met the Duke of Buckingham, with whom he had been in contact. Later chroniclers say that Buckingham was the first to contact Gloucester after the death of Edward IV, with, in the light of subsequent events, some implication that they were plotting together. Mancini thought that the first to contact Richard was Lord Hastings. It seems most likely that both men were in touch with Richard out of self-interest, as he would obviously be a major player in events, whatever happened.[5]

Meanwhile King Edward V, with his agreed escort of 2,000 men, together with Lord Rivers and his household, had left Ludlow on 24 April after celebrating the Garter ceremonies on the previous day.[6] Instead of heading directly for London (as Gloucester was), they deviated northwards towards the route being taken by the duke, and must thus have known roughly where he was expecting to be in the next few days, which implies that they had been in touch with each other as Mancini says. Thus Rivers and the king camped outside Stony Stratford in Buckinghamshire, probably on 29 April, just as Gloucester arrived in Northampton. Leaving the king in charge of his household, Rivers and his nephew, the queen's second son Richard Grey (also half-brother to the new king), went on to meet Gloucester and Buckingham just outside Northampton. Here they all seem to have stayed the night. The next day they all left to join the king in Stony Stratford, and it was probably while they were en route to Stony Stratford that Rivers and Grey were arrested and later sent to Richard's northern castles. The Dukes of Gloucester and Buckingham posted guards to prevent news of the arrests reaching the king's men, and then went to the king himself. They greeted him with the reverence due to his position but then arrested other members of his retinue, including Sir Richard Haute, the Controller of his Household, and Sir Thomas Vaughan, his Chamberlain. The dukes explained these arrests to the king by saying that they knew that men about the king had plotted against Richard's honour and life and furthermore were intending to deprive him of the position of Protector that was due to him by the wishes of his brother, the late King Edward IV. Edward apparently protested that his ministers had been selected for him by the king his father and that he trusted them. He seems in the end to have acquiesced in the situation; in fact, he could do little else. Gloucester then told his household, and presumably the 2,000 troops, to disperse. Without their leaders, the men dispersed quietly.[7] What really lay behind this coup is not clear. Much has been written about it from many points of view, ranging from this being the first move in a long-term plan by Gloucester to seize the throne – a theme favoured by the Tudor chroniclers and early historians – to the argument that Gloucester was merely protecting the young king from his wicked relatives. It seems very unlikely that the duke had at this stage any thoughts that he would or should take the throne, and the most likely explanation for his actions is that he was alarmed by the letters which Hasting had been sending him describing the actions of the Woodvilles in London, as a result of which he believed that his own safety and position were being threatened. Of course, once he had made this move against Rivers it can be argued that he had started a process that inevitably ended in him taking the throne himself, but that is to argue from hindsight, as what was going to happen was certainly not clear to the actors at the time.[8]

After the arrest of the king's attendants, the two dukes took the king back to Northampton, where they stayed for a few days. Official business was carried on here by Gloucester acting in the king's name. For example, he wrote to the Archbishop of Canterbury asking him to take control of the Great Seal (perhaps the duke had doubts about the reliability of the Chancellor, the Archbishop of York), the Tower of London and the treasure there. Interestingly, it was already too late for the latter, as will be seen. The king even took the trouble to write to ask the Bishop of Hereford to install one John Geffrey as priest in a church in his diocese.[9]. This letter is in fact dated 5 May but was sent from St Albans. Perhaps the date here should be 3 May and the royal party travelled to London via St Albans. Gloucester wrote in his own name to the Mayor of London and to the London city council. In these letters he explained that he had not arrested the king but had taken him into his own care to provide for the safety of the king and the kingdom, and that he had the greatest concern for both. He promised to bring the king to London very soon for him to be crowned. These letters were generally well received but understandably perhaps rumours began to circulate that the duke's real intention was to seize the crown.[10]

On 4 May the king arrived in London accompanied by 500 men, the joint entourages of the Dukes of Buckingham and Gloucester; at 'Harnsey park' just outside the city, he was joined by the city dignitaries wearing their red robes, and by liverymen of the major companies in murrey-coloured robes. The king was dressed in a blue velvet robe, and the Dukes of Gloucester and Buckingham in black to show they were in mourning for the late king. At the head of the procession were four cartloads of weapons bearing the devices of the queen's brothers and sons, which were proclaimed as having been stored outside London for use in attacking Gloucester as he entered the city. Some citizens were sceptical about this, believing that these weapons had in fact been stockpiled for the war against Scotland. Whatever the truth of the matter, it seems unlikely that weapons prepared for a contingency from at least a year before would still be there and not have been taken back to the armoury at the Tower.[11] After his entry into the city, the king went to the palace of the Bishop of London near St Pauls, the usual lodging for monarchs when in London. A few days after their arrival in the capital, Gloucester arranged for the city authorities and 'lords Spiritual and Temporall' to swear the oath of fealty to the king.[12]

At some time shortly after the arrival of the dukes and the king, the royal council went into a session lasting several days. There was much to discuss. A new date for the coronation was agreed. It was to be held on 22 June and Parliament was to be summoned for three days later. Just as importantly for the Duke of Gloucester, he was confirmed as Protector of the Realm, apparently with powers to act as tutor and governor to the king without the need to consult the council, as had been the case with previous holders of the office, 'commanding and forbidding in everything like another king', as the Crowland Chronicler describes it. It also appears that he was proposing to go against precedent and to remain Protector after the king had been crowned, when normally the office ceased. The speech drafted by Bishop Russell, the new Chancellor, for the opening of the Parliament summoned to meet on 25 June suggested that it was seemly for the king and his Protector to work together until the king came of age, probably at 15 years of age. Presumably Parliament was expected to confirm this novel arrangement.[13] The Protector also attempted to get the council to agree to the condemnation for treason of the men he had arrested at Stony Stratford, but the other councillors argued that since Gloucester then did not hold a public office, Rivers and the rest could not have committed treason. This was a strict interpretation of the Statute of Treason, in that Gloucester was not strictly speaking Rivers' lawful superior by office and it is interesting that the councillors insisted on following the letter of the law while Gloucester himself, who had a reputation for probity and as king proclaimed the importance of the rule of law, tried to ignore it.[14] However, the council seem to have agreed that Rivers, Grey and Vaughan should be kept in custody.

On 10 May John Russell, Bishop of Lincoln and a highly respected man, was appointed Lord Chancellor in the place of Thomas Rotherham, Archbishop of York. Other officers of state were also changed and Lord Hastings, who had been a great friend of Edward IV, was apparently confirmed in his offices of Lord Chamberlain (of the Household) and probably Captain of Calais too, but he had to wait for confirmation of his role as Master of the Mint until 20 May.[15] At this time the first moves were made against the queen's brother Sir Edward Woodville, who was at sea with a fleet and apparently had part of the late king's treasury with him. The explanation for this takes us back to 30 April/1 May, when the queen heard that Gloucester had arrested her brother Earl Rivers and her son Richard Grey. There is some confusion about what happened then in London but Mancini says that Queen Elizabeth and her eldest son Marquess Dorset tried to raise men to defend themselves and release the king from Gloucester's custody. However, when they asked the nobles present in the city to supply troops, they found that none of them would do so. As a result of this rebuff, the queen with her daughters and Richard, Duke of York, younger brother of the new king, and Marquess Dorset, together with her adherents, retreated into sanctuary in Westminster Abbey. The author of the Crowland Chronicle says that the queen and her family all went immediately into sanctuary without trying to raise troops to oppose Gloucester.[16] Mancini points out that the queen had fled to the Westminster sanctuary 12 years earlier while Edward IV was briefly in exile, and that her son Edward, now king, had been born there. It seems unlikely that they would have thought seriously of opposing Gloucester by armed force or could have believed that anyone would support them in doing so. He had made no overtly hostile actions towards anyone but the

Woodvilles, the queen's unpopular family, and most people doubtless would have waited to see how matters developed before taking any action. Dorset later escaped from sanctuary, probably in the summer since Mancini describes Richard as surrounding the grown crops in the neighbourhood (of the sanctuary) with troops and dogs. Nevertheless, Dorset evaded them all and took part in the later uprising in the autumn.[17]

Mancini reports that when the queen fled to sanctuary she and her brother Sir Edward Woodville and her eldest son Marquess Dorset divided the late king's treasure between them. Sir Edward had been commissioned by the council to gather a fleet and to sail to combat the French under the Sire D'Esquerdes (whom the English called Lord Cordis), who were harassing the coasts and detaining Englishmen. Sir Edward sailed on about 30 April or 1 May, perhaps before the news of Gloucester's coup had reached London, but he apparently took his share of the treasure with him. His commission had been given before Gloucester had started to play any part in the council deliberations and the Dukes of Gloucester and Buckingham can have had no idea what was happening. As seen above, Gloucester wrote to the Archbishop of Canterbury asking him *inter alia* to secure the treasure in the Tower. This was probably no more than a sensible precaution and not because he had any suspicion that it was seriously at risk.[18]

Sir Edward Woodville was obviously a threat that had to be dealt with. He had apparently not set out after the French ships but was anchored in the Downs off the east coast of Kent. Here he was dangerous and he needed to be neutralised as soon as possible. It was agreed that everyone in the fleet except for Sir Edward himself, Marquess Dorset (who Richard obviously believed was with his uncle), and one Robert Ratcliff would all receive a pardon if they would submit. This message was sent out to Woodville's fleet by a small flotilla of ships led by two experienced commanders, Thomas Fulford and Sir Edward Brampton. The promise of a pardon worked for most of the men in the fleet, and some of Woodville's ships sailed away under the command of their foreign merchant owners, who certainly did not want to offend the ruling powers in England, but Sir Edward managed to escape with two of his ships and his treasure and took refuge in Brittany, where he joined Henry Tudor, calling himself Earl of Richmond.[19] Tudor was the Lancastrian claimant to the throne, although his claim was tenuous. The son of Owen Tudor and Margaret Beaufort, daughter of John Beaufort, Duke of Somerset, his claim derived from his mother's position as the heiress of the Beauforts, who were descended from John of Gaunt, Duke of Lancaster. The Beauforts were an illegitimate line, although legitimised by Henry IV, and Tudor and his mother were the only Lancastrian claimants left. Tudor had been brought up in England but fled to Brittany under the tutelage of his uncle Jasper after the collapse of the Lancastrian restoration of 1469–1470. The Duke of Brittany had taken them into his protection, and they remained there for the next twelve years. Little is known about their lives in Brittany. They were of little political importance, although Edward IV sporadically tried to get them back into his custody. It was only when Richard of Gloucester became king that Tudor became more valuable, both to the Duke of Brittany and to other foreign powers, as a possible lever to use against the new king. It is difficult to see where else Edward Woodville could have gone, but his decision to take refuge in Brittany and the fact that he took part of Edward IV's treasure to Tudor might indicate that this was part of a plan devised by the queen and her party in the first place.

Three or four days after the changes and confirmations of new offices on 10 May, another group from what seems to have been the inner circle of barons supporting Gloucester in London was rewarded. This group included William Hastings, the Earl of Arundel and John, Lord Howard. Howard was a long-term Yorkist supporter and one of Gloucester's colleagues in the Scots expedition of 1481. He was obviously helping Gloucester at this difficult time and he was now rewarded for his support, initially with the lucrative office of the Chief Steward of the Duchy of Lancaster south of the Trent. Howard showed his gratitude for this on 15 May by giving to the Protector a massive gold cup weighing 65 ounces, a very valuable gift.[20] On the same day the Duke of Buckingham, whom Mancini described as being 'always at hand to assist Gloucester with his advice and resources', received rewards for this support in the form of spectacular and entirely unprecedented rewards. He was made Chief Justice and Chamberlain in both north and south Wales for life, with very full powers to array men in the border counties, as well as being appointed Constable and Steward of all of the castles and lordships in Wales and the marches and being granted supervision and governance of all the king's subjects in the same areas. Such a concentration of power in the hands of one man was risky, no matter how much he was trusted by Gloucester.[21]

At about this time (it was recent news when Simon Stallworth mentioned it on 9 June) young Edward was moved from the Bishop of London's palace to the Tower of London to await his coronation. The Tower then was a royal palace and had no sinister reputation such as it later acquired in the sixteenth century. Preparations for the coronation were still being made and on 20 May letters were sent to the sheriffs of each county ordering them to proclaim that all those within their areas who were not knights but had the financial qualifications to be so should present themselves to receive the order of knighthood before the king by 18 June. On 5 June the king wrote again to some 50 gentlemen who had obviously been identified as suitable for knighthood and summoned them to appear to be knighted at his coronation, which was to be held on 22 June.[22] By 5 June, therefore, it appears that events were still going steadily forward for Edward V to be crowned as planned on the revised date of 22 June. The Duchess of Gloucester arrived in London on this day, obviously to be in time to attend the coronation.[23]

The writs for the Parliament which was to meet on 25 June had been sent out by 3 June, because the city of London's common council met on that day and duly elected their four representatives to attend on their behalf.[24] On 6 June the city authorities in York received their writ to elect their parliamentary representatives, unusually for four MPs instead of two. Nearly a week later, on 13 June, the York council decided that the same men should attend the coronation and then remain in London for the Parliament three days later. Only two men are mentioned at this point, so it appears that the numbers had been sorted out. These two men were to be allowed wages for eight days to go to London for this purpose.[25]

However, in London by this date all was not going smoothly towards the coronation, and although the York city fathers did not know it, the Yorkshire knight Sir Richard Ratcliffe was already galloping towards them with a desperate appeal from Gloucester (describing himself as 'brother and uncle of kings, Protector, Defender, Great Chamberlain, Constable and Admiral of England) for help with as many men as they could gather to 'aid and assist us against the queen, her blood adherents and affinity', who 'intended and daily do intend to murder and utterly destroy us and our cousin the Duke of Buckingham and the old royal blood of this realm', as well as destroying and disinheriting Gloucester's adherents in the north. This letter, dated 10 June, arrived in York on 15 June and the council decided to send 200 men south immediately. The dire wording may have galvanised them into a speedy decision, although implementing the decision took a little longer. The next day they increased the force by another 100 men and reached agreement about pay and equipment, with each man paying for his own jacket. How to muster the troops took another five days of discussion. A proclamation from the Duke of Gloucester to the same effect as the letter was made on 19 June, and by 21 June the York councillors had decided that their troops should join up with the Earl of Northumberland, who had also been summoned, at Pontefract and that they should wear the badge of the city and Gloucester's boar. On 21 June they received the writ of *supesedeas* cancelling the Parliament of 25 June, so their intended parliamentary representatives were sent to London in command of the troops instead.[26] Given this delay, if the Duke of Gloucester had really needed the troops in a great hurry they would not have been a great deal of use. Quite why he wrote to the city asking for these men, knowing that they might not arrive for two weeks at best, has been much discussed. He had also sent a letter by Ratcliffe, this one dated 11 June, to his cousin Lord Neville, who was probably at Raby castle in County Durham, asking him also to come to London 'defensibly arrayed', and there may have been similar letters to others in the north.[27] The most likely explanation for Gloucester's request for help from his northern supporters (who he knew would respond positively) is that he did not expect any serious opposition in the near future, although he obviously expected something to happen at some point. It has been suggested that the troops were intended to arrive after the coronation of Edward V on 22 June, which would explain York's delay in implementing the Protector's request, reflecting verbal orders transmitted via Ratcliffe. The troops would then be available to help maintain Gloucester as Protector in case of opposition after the coronation.[28]

The most obvious explanation for the request for troops is that by this time Gloucester knew that he would take the throne but did not know at this stage when he would need support. It may be that he decided to take this course when Robert Stillington, Bishop of Bath and Wells, informed him that Edward IV had already been pre-contracted to one Eleanor Butler when he had married Elizabeth Woodville. This would render Elizabeth's children, including Edward V, illegitimate and thus unable to inherit honours, including the throne. Much has been said about this and debate has long raged over whether or not Stillington made any such claim and if he did, whether it would have had the effect described, but for present purposes it is sufficient to say that actions were taken which were seemingly based on a belief that Stillington's story was true. Certainly it seems that it was during this time that Richard made up his mind to take the throne.[29]

On Friday, 13 June there occurred an event that probably hastened the Protector's final step to the throne. At a council meeting that day Richard angrily accused Lord Hastings, who seemed to have been acting in every way to support the Protector, of plotting against his life. Hastings was arrested and summarily executed, apparently without trial. Others, including the Archbishop of York, John Morton, Bishop of Ely, and Thomas, Lord Stanley were also arrested as being part of the plot. Mancini says that Hastings was killed by Richard's men, while the Crowland Chronicler merely says that he was executed by order of the Protector.[30] Whatever happened, the effect must have been dramatic. The Dukes of Buckingham and Gloucester sent out messengers immediately to proclaim that a plot had been detected, and that its originator, Hastings, had been executed. We are told that men were initially reassured but later people began to say that the plot was little more than a ruse by the Protector to get rid of the new king's strongest supporters. There may well have been such a plot, and presumably the council supported Gloucester in his actions, perhaps reluctantly, but it is difficult to avoid the conclusion that

Gloucester deliberately eliminated Hastings because he knew he would have remained loyal to Edward V, and he would have been the natural leader of Edward IV's household men in any subsequent rebellion against Richard.[31] Two days later, on 16 June, Gloucester acted to remove the Duke of York from sanctuary in Westminster, where he had been since the queen fled there with her family on the news of the arrest of her brother Rivers. If the king was to be crowned in just over a week, it was absurd that his brother should remain in sanctuary. Westminster was duly ringed with troops and the Archbishop of Canterbury and Russell, the Lord Chancellor, with other lords, went in to talk to the queen. She was persuaded that it would be better for the king and his brother to be together and the queen agreed, and after being greeted by Gloucester 'with many loving words' in the Star Chamber in Westminster Palace, the young duke was escorted to the Tower to join his brother the king. The queen still refused to come out of sanctuary herself, nor would she allow her daughters to do so.[32] Writs were issued on this same day or the next postponing the Parliament and delaying the coronation of Edward V until 9 November.[33]

Rumours of troops approaching from the north had reached London on or before 21 June and extra watches were set in the streets. The men from York would not have arrived yet since they did not set out until 21 June, as seen above, but since they were mounted the journey would not have taken long. The number of troops was greatly exaggerated, of course (at 20,000 instead of the actual 300), as these things usually were, but would be the more alarming for that.[34] On 22 June, a Sunday, a sermon was preached by Ralph Shaa, brother of the Lord Mayor of London, at St Paul's Cross. His text was 'Bastard slips shall not take root', and his words alleged the bastardy of the children of Edward IV and emphasised the undoubted legitimacy of the Duke of Gloucester's claim to the throne. A few days later, probably on 25 June, the day originally appointed for the meeting of Parliament, Lord Rivers, his brother Richard Grey and Thomas Vaughan were executed in Pontefract castle on the authority of the Protector, perhaps without trial, although Rous the chronicler says that the Earl of Northumberland was their chief judge.[35] The order for their execution must have been sent several days earlier and was an act that could only have been arranged by a king or by someone who expected to be a king. The Crowland Chronicler says that the order to execute them was carried by Sir Richard Ratcliffe as he travelled to London with the northern troops.[36] Obviously, if Ratcliffe had carried the order up from London when he left on 11 June, then the decision to execute Rivers and his colleagues must had been taken long before.

On the day before the executions of Rivers, Grey and Vaughan, the Duke of Buckingham addressed a group of leading city of London citizens on the suitability of the Duke of Gloucester to be king, on the grounds of the illegitimacy of Edward V and his brother.[37] On the next day an informal gathering of Lords Temporal and Spiritual and commoners in a kind of *ad hoc* parliament presented to the Duke of Gloucester a petition that set out his title to the throne and asked him to become king. The text of this petition is generally thought to be the same as that in the bill presented in Parliament some months later, which also set out Richard's claim to the throne (see below, p. 27). The 1483 petition repeated the claim of the Duke of Buckingham that Edward V was illegitimate. The Crowland Chronicler said that it declared that Edward V and his brother, and by extension all the children of Edward IV and Elizabeth Woodville, were illegitimate on the grounds that Edward had been pre-contracted to one Eleanor Butler and his marriage was therefore invalid. Since George, Duke of Clarence (Richard's elder brother) had been attainted, his children were unable to claim the throne and so Richard was the sole heir of Richard, Duke of York (the father of Edward IV, George and Richard) with a valid claim to the throne. The Chronicler ends by saying, 'At the end of this roll therefore, on behalf of the lords and commonalty of the kingdom, he was besought to assume his lawful rights'. Richard duly agreed and he was escorted to Westminster Hall where he was dressed in royal robes and took his seat on the marble throne in the court of King's Bench. The new king made a speech to the assembled judges, asking them to administer justice impartially and declaring that he regarded the administration of the law to be the chief duty of the king. His actions during his reign showed that to a great extent he lived up to this. He further declared that he would date his reign from that day, 26 June.

Richard III then heard a Te Deum in Westminster Abbey and was escorted back to the city of London where he was greeted by the authorities.[38]

On the next day, 27 June, the new king gave the great seal to the Bishop of Lincoln, confirming him in the office he had held under Edward V. On the next day Richard's supporters received their reward. Buckingham was made Great Chamberlain, giving him oversight of most of the arrangements for the coronation and John Howard was made Duke of Norfolk and Earl Marshal of England, titles to which he had a claim through his mother, a member of the Mowbray family. These were titles that had been held by Prince Richard, but presumably the new king decided that the special circumstances under which Prince Richard had been created Duke of Norfolk on his marriage to the Mowbray heiress (who had died not long after the marriage) were no longer valid. There is no doubt that Prince Richard was still alive at this time. Lord Berkeley was at the same time created Earl of Nottingham, another Mowbray title. Howard's son Thomas was created Earl of Surrey on the same day as his father was made duke. Soon after this, the new Duke of Norfolk was made High Steward of England and was appointed to hear claims on 3 July to perform duties at the coronation. The proceedings of this Court of Claims must have been held very speedily since the date of the coronation had been set for 6 July.[39] On about 3 July the troops from York seem to have arrived in London, rather to the alarm of the citizens. Together with the troops brought by Gloucester and Buckingham when they entered London in May, they were encamped outside the city, perhaps in Finsbury or Moorgate Fields. The equipment of the newly arrived York men was derided by the Londoners and the city and the king made regulations to ensure that the peace was kept.[40]

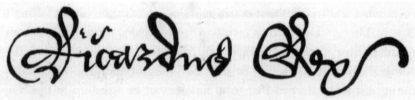

The signature of Richard III. (*Geoffrey Wheeler*)

Chapter 1

The New King

On 6 July 1483 Richard of Gloucester was duly crowned King of England as Richard III. His wife Anne was crowned with him, the first double coronation for 175 years, since that of Edward II and Isabelle of France. The splendid coronation was attended by most of the nobility of England and a great throng of the gentry, and those playing a major part on the day included those who supported Richard throughout his reign and in his final battle as well as those who became his enemies.

On the day of the coronation Richard was dressed by his Great Chamberlain, the Duke of Buckingham, who would also play a part supporting the king in the subsequent ceremony. Together with the queen and various nobles, they then made their way to Westminster Hall, where they were joined by the abbot and monks of Westminster, the dean of the Chapel Royal and the bishops, headed by the Archbishop of Canterbury, Richard's elderly distant cousin Thomas Bourchier. They formed up in a long procession and walked the short distance to the west door of Westminster Abbey. The carriers of the royal regalia were allies and relatives of the new king: John Howard, created Duke of Norfolk eight days before, carried St Edward's crown, while his son the Earl of Surrey carried the sword of state. Richard's uncle, the Earl of Essex, carried the gilt spurs, and his brother-in-law the Duke of Suffolk carried the royal sceptre and Suffolk's eldest son, the Earl of Lincoln, the orb. A political ally carrying part of the regalia was Lord Lovell, who carried the third sword of justice. Those whom Richard hoped would prove to be his political allies included the Earl of Northumberland carrying Curtana, the point-less sword of mercy, and Thomas, Lord Stanley carrying the constable's mace. After the coronation the procession returned to

Westminster Hall, and the king and queen rested while the hall was prepared for the banquet that was to follow. This was a splendid affair. It started at 1 pm on a bright summer's day, and went on for so long that the last course (of three) was not served as darkness had already fallen. The banquet must therefore have lasted about 7 hours. All must have been exhausted by the end.

Richard was doubtless as tired as anyone but an event such as a coronation was an opportunity to reward friends and bind in allies, and he must have hoped and believed that he had done all that he could that day to bring people to his side. In the following week the traditional jousts were probably held, but it is unlikely that Richard would have had time to pay a great deal of attention to them. His attention was concentrated on consolidating his position.[1] He spent two weeks at Greenwich, moving later to Windsor, doing such necessary things as informing the Kings of France and Castile of his accession and issuing patents to further reward his friends. In addition to his powerful offices in Wales and the marches (which were confirmed by the new king), the Duke of Buckingham was made Constable of England, an office to which he had a hereditary right. The Duke of Norfolk was made Admiral of England, an office held by Richard until his accession. Buckingham was also granted many manors.[2] On 19 July a patent was issued creating Edward, Richard's only legitimate son, Lord Lieutenant of Ireland for three years. This post had become that usually held by the heirs of the Yorkist kings. Edward, or his father on his behalf, promptly granted the deputy lieutenancy to the Earl of Kildare, one of the most powerful men in Ireland[3]

On 21 July the king left Windsor accompanied by a train of bishops, lords and household officers to go on a progress of his realm to show himself to his people and buttress his authority. He went first to Oxford, where at his own request he heard disputations in several colleges, and then on to Gloucester, where as a compliment to the city whose name he had borne he made it a county in its own right. From here he went to Warwick, which he reached on 8 August. Here he was joined by Queen Anne. He stayed in Warwick for one week, during which he gave an audience to an ambassador from Queen Isabella of Castille. It has been suggested, following Rous, that this ambassador, Geoffrey de Sasiola, proposed the marriage of Prince Edward and Isabella, the daughter of King Ferdinand and Queen Isabella. This seems unlikely, since no such marriage is mentioned in Richard's letter to his council in London written on 9 August, presumably after his conversation with de Sasiola, in which he merely said that a treaty of amity had been proposed, and one should be drawn up if they so agreed. Nor was such a marriage mentioned in his message written on 12 September (while he was in York) to his envoy to Spain, in which he instructed him to renew the old treaty or negotiate a new one as Queen Isabella wished.[4] From Warwick, Richard and Anne went to Pontefract, arriving about 24 August. Here they were joined by Prince Edward, who had apparently left Middleham two days before as his household expenses were paid up to 22 August at Middleham.[5]

It seems likely that the young prince met his parents on 24 August, the date of his formal creation as Prince of Wales and Earl of Chester. The charter granting these titles to 'our dearest first born son Edward' praises the prince highly, saying that the 'outstanding qualities with which he is singularly endowed for his age give great, and by the favour of God, undoubted hope of future uprightness'. It would be pleasant to think that these phrases are not merely conventional and represent a genuine expression of esteem. The prince was never officially created Duke of Cornwall, although he was considered to hold that title since he is thus named in a number of official documents (for example when he was summoned to Parliament in December).[6]

After a short stay at Pontefract, the royal party moved on to York, arriving on 29 August. Preparations for their arrival had been going on in York since at least the end of July, when a resolution was made to meet the king at Breckles Mills just outside the city, and the deliberations of the council for the next month were about little else. These preparations were not entirely chosen by the council. John Kendall, secretary to the king, wrote to the city fathers from Nottingham on 23 August, advising them to receive the king and queen 'as honourably as your wisdoms can imagine', and further, to hang the streets through which they were to pass with cloth of arras and tapestry work, 'for there come many southern

Lords and men of worship with them which will mark greatly your receiving their graces'. It was true that a visit by such an important group did not occur often. With the king and queen and Prince Edward were the Bishops of Durham, Worcester, St Asaph, Carlisle and St Davids, the Duke of Albany (brother of the King of Scotland), the Earls of Northumberland, Lincoln, Surrey (Steward of the King's Household) and Warwick (son of the Duke of Clarence), Lords Stanley, Strange, Fitz Hugh, Lisle and Greystoke, Francis, Lord Lovell, Chamberlain of the king, and Sir William Hussey, the Lord Chief Justice.[7]

The visit to York was indeed memorable. As the royal party approached the city on 29 August, it was met at Tadcaster by the two sheriffs, each bearing their rods of office, who rode at the head of the procession. One of the sheriffs was too ill to perform this duty, and a deputy stood in for him. At Breckles Mills the royal party was met by the mayor and aldermen in their scarlet robes, and the city officers and leading citizens in red gowns. Passing St James's Church outside the Micklegate Bar, they were greeted by the citizens of York, with bridgemasters, former bridgemasters and 'other honest men' in red, and all 'other persons' in blue violet and musterdivilers (a kind of mixed grey woollen cloth). Inside the city, the streets of which were doubtless hung with the arras and tapestries requested by Kendall, three separate pageants were staged for the amusement of the king. These had been arranged by Henry Hudson, Rector of the Church of All Saints in North Street. He later received 40 shillings for his labours. At some point in the proceedings the mayor made a speech of welcome, and presented to the king 100 marks and to the queen 100 pounds of gold, both in rich pieces of plate. The king and his party then passed into the minster church, where they were received by the dean and clergy in their red copes and a service was held. After this they went on to the palace of the Archbishop, where they stayed.[8]

The warm welcome which he received in York seems to have persuaded Richard to hold the ceremonial investiture of his son as Prince of Wales while he was there. Arrangements had to be made quickly, and in fact took only one week. That the decision was a sudden one and not premeditated is shown by the fact that Richard had to send a message to Piers Curteys,

Keeper of the Great Wardrobe, in London for the necessary items.[9] The order to Curteys is dated 'the last day of August' and is immensely detailed, including clothing for some of those taking part in the procession, and also requesting no fewer than 13,000 cloth badges depicting the king's own symbol of the White Boar for distribution to the populace. Sir James Tyrell, Master of the King's Henchmen (and also Master of the Horse), and seven of the henchmen (pages) were given many yards of holland cloth and other materials 'for the noble creation of my Lord Prince'. The week occupied by the preparations was taken up by banquets and on the Sunday by a performance of the York Creed play before the royal party. On 3 October the council paid 10 marks to the mayor towards his expenses for two dinners held while the king was in the city.[10]

The day appointed for the ceremony was Monday, 8 September, the festival of the Nativity of the Blessed Virgin Mary. It was performed by the king, after an elaborate ceremonial display begun in the minster by the Bishop of Durham celebrating mass. The absence of Thomas Rotherham, Archbishop of York, from his own cathedral may be significant. After this ceremony, the king went crowned through the streets of the city, accompanied by a great number of nobles, and followed by the queen, also crowned and leading by the hand their son Edward wearing his coronet. The citizens in the crowded streets greeted the royal family with 'great honour, joy and congratulations as in show of rejoicing they extolled King Richard above the skies'. The royal party then returned to the Archbishop's Palace, where the king invested his son as Prince of Wales, in the presence of the whole court. He girded on the sword, presented him with the golden rod and ring, and placed a garland on his head, insignia of his rank. Later Richard created his son a knight, together with his nephew the Earl of Warwick, his illegitimate son John of Gloucester and the Spanish ambassador de Sasiola.[11]

Nine days later on 17 September Richard displayed his gratitude to the city of York for his reception by calling before him to the chapter house of the minster the mayor, the aldermen and the commoners of the city. He thanked them for their services to him and, without any prompting on their part (a point stressed in the York records), granted them relief of more than half the taxes which they paid to the crown. This meant that non-residents coming into the city would henceforth not have to pay any tolls to do so. Richard also made the mayor one of his chief sergeants-at-arms, with a wage of a shilling per day. Other business transacted during this week was on behalf of the Prince of Wales. His tenants in the Principality were ordered to pay their taxes and to attend before the agents appointed by the Duke of Buckingham as Justiciar and Chamberlain of North and South Wales. On the same day the king also sent a letter to Sir William Stanley, Chamberlain of the County Palatine of Chester, ordering him on behalf of the prince to have engraved a new great seal for the county. At the same time Buckingham at least was planning a dangerous revolt against Richard, although Sir William was probably not at this time.[12] This progress has been dealt with at length because in some ways it marks the high point of Richard's monarchy, the point at which he must have felt that his realm was at peace and that he had done all he could to make himself accepted by his subjects.

The royal party probably left York soon after these events, probably on 20 or 21 September. They went directly from York to Pontefract, the king still being accompanied by his wife and son. They stayed at Pontefract for more than two weeks, before the king left for Gainsborough. At Lincoln on 11 October the king learned of Buckingham's revolt. He quickly wrote to his friends in York, telling them that the Duke of Buckingham had turned traitor and asking them once again to send him as many mounted troops as they could raise quickly to aid him against this new threat. The city council duly ordered the raising of 200 armed men to be at Leicester by 21 October as requested. Richard also wrote to the Chancellor from Lincoln asking him to send (or to bring) the Great Seal. He explained that he intended 'to advance us towards our rebel and traitor the Duke of Buckingham to resist and withstand his malicious purpose'. In a postscript in his own hand Richard added bitterly, 'Here loved be God is all well and truly determined and for to resist the malice of him that had best cause to be true the Duke of Buckingham the most untrue creature living whom with Gods good grace we shall not be long till that we will be in that part and subdue his malice. We assure you that there was never false traitor better purveyed for'. On 15 October Richard issued a proclamation against Buckingham condemning him in similar bitter terms. This language displays his shock, horror and moral outrage at Buckingham's action.[13] It seems apparent that Richard was not expecting any such action on Buckingham's part; indeed, why should he? Much has been said about this issue, but the most likely suggestion seems to be that Buckingham was originally aiming for the throne himself, since he had a distant claim through Thomas of Woodstock, the youngest son of Edward III. Before this went very far, though, Buckingham must have discovered that a large plot was under way to free the two princes and restore Edward V to the throne. This was being organised largely by disgruntled former supporters and household men of Edward IV. A rumour that the princes were dead seems to have overtaken this plan and it was replaced by another to raise to the throne Henry Tudor, the Lancastrian claimant, with the intention that he should marry Elizabeth, the eldest daughter of Edward IV, and thus unite the two competing factions. This new plan, a 'coalition of all hostile elements' as it has been called, was also supported by the Woodville faction and by Margaret Beaufort, mother of Henry Tudor. The instigator of this plan is usually said to have been John Morton, Bishop of Ely, who had been arrested at the council meeting after which Lord Hastings was executed. He had been sent to Brecon castle, in the custody of the Duke of Buckingham. Morton was an ally of Margaret Beaufort, wife of Lord Stanley, who was also arrested briefly on the same occasion.[14] We will never know whether or not Buckingham wholeheartedly endorsed the plan to put Henry Tudor on the throne, but he may have calculated that his own best interests were served by at least supporting the plan for now and settling the question of who was to replace Richard when they had succeeded in deposing him. He certainly wrote to Tudor and to his uncle Jasper in Brittany as early as 24 September, encouraging him to assemble a fleet and soldiers and to invade England.[15]

The risings intended to accomplish the plan were largely southern-based, and it was the rising in early October of the Kentish men who proclaimed that the Duke of Buckingham was their leader that alerted Richard and his supporters to what was afoot. According to the act of attainder passed after the event, the original date when these events began was 18 October for the rising in the south-east with other dates assigned to other sectors. Around that date there were certainly risings at various centres in the south. By then the Duke of Norfolk had blocked the Kentish men from crossing the Thames by placing men at the Gravesend crossing. This frustrated their plan to link up with an uprising in Essex. Howard also used his own household men to protect London, having begun summoning them as early as 10 October. This destabilised this part of the rebellion.[16]

Meanwhile the troops summoned by the king and the other lords travelling with him gathered at Leicester as ordered, although not all of the expected men arrived. Lord Lovell, for example, wrote to his retainer Sir William Stonor asking him to bring as many men as he could to Leicester by 20 October. Other men summoned by Lovell were to gather at Banbury on 18 October, whence Lovell would go to Leicester. However, Stonor would not be marching with troops to the king's aid since he had already sided with Buckingham and was later attainted for it. The Duke of Norfolk similarly wrote on 10 October to John Paston, his tenant, telling him that 'the Kentishmen be up in the weald and say that they will come and rob the city which I shall let if I may' (if that is what the Kentish men were really saying, then it does not sound as if they had strong feelings about the sons of Edward IV or indeed other political matters) and asking Paston to bring 'six tall fellows in harness'. Whether they came or not is not known. This may have happened frequently at this time, as men's allegiances were not necessarily known and their support was uncertain. Some parts of the country had messengers coming both from the king and from the Duke of Buckingham to encourage men to support the writers. This certainly applied to Lancaster and the Stanley family, who this time came down on the side of the king.[17] More regular methods for gathering troops were also used. Lovell, for example, received a general commission of array 'for the resistance of the rebel Henry Duke of Buckingham' on 23 October. The commission of array (see Appendix 2) was the usual method at this time to raise troops at short notice for the defence of the realm (as opposed to foreign wars). Unusually, and presumably to save time, the patent for Lovell's commission was issued by verbal order of the king and not, as usual, by privy seal writ.[18]

After writing from Lincoln to the men of York, the king had travelled to Grantham, where he received the Great Seal he had requested from the Lord Chancellor. He then returned to Leicester on 22 October, where he took command of the gathered troops. From here he marched to Oxford. It seems probable that here, or perhaps before this, he had information from Norfolk that he was containing the eastern and southern part of the risings and so Richard swung to the southwest to deal with Buckingham. In fact, Buckingham's endeavours had not prospered. He had apparently unfurled his banners on 18 October but his subsequent progress had not been a triumph. His rear had been harassed by the Vaughans of Tretower, who had even taken the duke's own castle of Brecon, and ahead of him Humphrey Stafford had destroyed the bridges over the Severn, denying him access to England. This situation was made worse by the Severn being in flood after the most tremendous gales and rainstorms in the middle of October had flooded the West Country and all the river crossings.[19] The duke was forced to halt his march at Weobley. The delay proved fatal to his hopes and his army melted away. The duke himself fled northwards into Shropshire, where he apparently took refuge with Ralph Banaster, one of his retainers. After a few days Banaster betrayed him to the sheriff of the county and Buckingham was taken to Salisbury, arriving there on 1 November.

Richard arrived there at about the same time, probably having arranged the rendezvous as soon as he heard of the collapse of Buckingham's rebellion and his capture. The duke was tried immediately before the court of the Vice Constable. Buckingham himself was Constable of England, but Richard had already appointed Sir Ralph Assheton as Vice Constable on 24 October with all the necessary powers to try cases of treason 'without formalities or appeal'. Buckingham was executed in the market square in Salisbury on the next day, All Souls Day, 2 November. Banaster, his betrayer, was rewarded by the grant of the manor of Yalding in Kent, worth £50 per year. This was much less than the reward promised for the apprehension of Buckingham in Richard's proclamation from Leicester on 23 October, which had offered £1,000 or lands worth £100 per year.[20] Buckingham's death coincided with the collapse of the other risings in the south. These had taken place at various locations, including Maidstone, Guildford and Salisbury, but none had individually been important, and would only have become so had the main thrust of the rebellion led by Buckingham succeeded.

After Buckingham's execution, Richard pressed on south until he reached the coast at Bridport. It seems likely that Henry Tudor had attempted a landing near here at Poole with two ships of troops. He had been loaned a large sum of money by Francis, Duke of Brittany, who also paid for the provisions he needed and the wages of the men he took with him. We do not know how many men there were, but Vergil says they numbered 5,000. At least seven ships set out, manned by 515 men. These ships had assembled in early September, well before Buckingham's letter could have been received, and sailed about the end of October from the port of Paimpol in Brittany, but were scattered by the same gales that ruined Buckingham's enterprise. Vergil says that Tudor with two ships found himself off Poole at dawn at about the time Richard was in Salisbury. Suspecting that all was not well with the rebel enterprise, despite calls from the troops on the shore that Buckingham's army was advancing to the coast to join up with him, Tudor sailed on to Plymouth. Here he heard that the king was in the vicinity with his army and so he returned to Brittany. Here he was joined by the leaders of the western end of the rising, including Elizabeth Woodville's son the Marquess of Dorset, and her brother Lionel Woodville, Bishop of Salisbury.[21]

From Bridport Richard went westwards, to Exeter. Another section of the rebellion had occurred here, centred partly on Bodmin in Cornwall. The leaders included Piers Courtenay, Bishop of Exeter, and Edward Courtenay (later restored to the earldom of Devonshire by Henry VII), and this part of the rising seems to have started on 3 November and to have taken place in the name of Henry Tudor.[22] One of the West Country leaders was Sir Thomas St Leger, who was captured and executed on 13 November. He was Richard's brother-in-law, having married Richard's sister Anne, Duchess of Exeter. St Leger's son was contracted to marry

Dorset's daughter, with expectations of inheriting the Exeter estates. Richard spent a few days in Exeter and then returned slowly to London, via Bridgwater, Winchester and Guildford, probably to overawe by his presence any remaining pockets of disaffection. He entered London in triumph on 25 November, some seven weeks after first hearing of the uprisings and after a nearly bloodless campaign.

This rebellion had turned out to be less dangerous than it had at first appeared, largely because of Buckingham's failure to engage the royal army at all, partly due to the bad weather. Given his failure, and Tudor's inability to land all his forces (again largely because of the weather), the rebellion failed to strike a concerted blow, and the smaller risings were dealt with piecemeal by local forces. The whole rebellion thus failed due to a number of accidents, helped by Richard's resolute action. The real result was that the dangerously narrow power base of the new regime had been exposed, as many of those who had taken part in the uprising had formerly been strong supporters of the Yorkist regime under Edward IV, and Richard had retained them in local offices. That they did not support Richard may have been due to their distaste for the way he had taken the throne or perhaps because they believed he had murdered his nephews. Many of these disaffected men were from the south and when they fled to join Tudor in Brittany they left serious vacancies in the power structure in the south of England, as well as helping to strengthen Tudor's claim as a pretender to the throne. To replace them Richard was forced to rely on men from his northern power base. Placing such men in positions of authority in the south was very unpopular with the remaining gentry of the shires, who naturally resented the intrusion of outsiders. From this point on Richard's regime was in reality unstable and the rest of his reign was spent to a large extent in making preparations for the next uprising.[23]

After his efforts the king spent Christmas 1483 with great pomp, wearing his crown at Epiphany. He must have felt he should show that at last he felt secure on his throne. He apparently paid for the celebrations by selling some of the royal treasure.[24] Tudor was still in Brittany in exile, but on Christmas morning in Rennes cathedral he swore an oath before his supporters to marry Elizabeth, the eldest daughter of Edward IV, as soon as he should become king, thus leaving no doubt about his intentions. His followers knelt and swore homage as though he were already king.[25]

Even after the crushing of the uprising of 1483 the realm was not entirely quiet and the foreign situation remained difficult. Rumours of invasion never ceased. Before Christmas Richard had sent out commissions of array to most of the English counties, and stationed a fleet in the English Channel. Commanded by Sir Thomas Wentworth, the fleet had orders to guard the approaches to the south coast and to combat the Breton ships preying on English ships and causing problems for trade.[26] Henry Tudor was still based in Brittany and could be expected to make another descent on England as soon as conditions were right. Other ships were later equipped to guard other parts of the coast. In an effort to ease the unrest in some areas the king was busy sending out writs and instructions to various authorities. The Sheriff of Staffordshire was ordered to administer the oath of allegiance to everyone in his jurisdiction, and to strictly forbid the wearing of any livery or cognisances except the king's. The Chamberlain of North Wales was similarly ordered to administer the oath, and the Mayor of Gloucester to maintain the statutes against the taking of livery. He must have felt that the situation in Kent was still very disturbed, as he also wrote to the mayor and council of Canterbury ordering them to see that men wore no livery badges or cognisances except the king's, and he issued separate commissions to various parts of Kent to ensure that the men of Kent between the ages of 16 and 60 swore the oath of allegiance. This may have been an attempt to ensure that as many men as possible did so. In December Richard also made a proclamation in Kent against the known rebels, enjoining his subjects to make every effort to arrest them.[27]

In late January 1484 Richard's first – and only – Parliament met. The previous summer a Parliament had been called for 25 June, just after the proposed coronation of Edward V, but this was abandoned after the cancellation of the coronation. Another was summoned for 6 November but the Duke of Buckingham's uprising meant that this was called off as late as 2 November, so that most of the members would have been elected and already present in London. The writs for the Parliament that sat in January 1484 were sent out on 9 November. It met on 23 January 1484 and sat for nearly a month, being dissolved on 20 February. It passed a number of laws but its most important business was to pass the act known as Titulus Regius, the Title of the King.

The core of the bill presented to the Commons was the petition presented to Richard in June 1483 asking him to take the throne on the grounds that Edward IV's marriage to Elizabeth Woodville was invalid because of a pre-contract and his children therefore illegitimate, and that Richard was the family's sole legitimate heir, as explained above. However, the bill went on to say that because the estates who had originally presented the petition had not been formally part of a Parliament, it was considered best to rehearse the contents and ratify their truth. The rest of this bill set out the right of the king very comprehensively, and ended by declaring that the crown and all that pertained to it 'shall rest and remain in the person of our said sovereign lord the king during his life and after his death in his heirs begotten of his body and ... be it ordained ... that the high and excellent Prince Edward son of our said sovereign lord the king is heir apparent of our same sovereign lord the king' and would succeed him in all his rights after his death.[28] It was duly passed by the commons and lords, and while Parliament was still sitting was followed by another ceremony in which the lords and the leading household men took an oath of loyalty to the prince as Richard's heir.[29] This ceremony took place on a February afternoon while Parliament was in recess, and in a 'certain downstairs room near the corridor which leads to the queen's quarters'. The only person actually named by the Crowland Chronicler as being present was John Howard, Duke of Norfolk, but there is no doubt that on such a formal occasion many other lords and commons would have been present. There is no evidence that young Edward himself was present.

Perhaps over the Christmas period, and certainly while Parliament was sitting, negotiations were in progress with Elizabeth Woodville, who was still in sanctuary with her daughters; their Christmas must have been rather depressing. Their situation was obviously an embarrassment to the king and the negotiations were intended to secure the release of the daughters of Edward IV from sanctuary into Richard's guardianship. The negotiations bore fruit at the beginning of March, when Richard swore on the word of a king (*verbo regio*), before a group of the Lords Spiritual and Temporal, who were still in London after the ending of Parliament, as well as the mayor and aldermen of the city of London, that if the daughters of the late king would come out of sanctuary 'and be guided, ruled and demeaned by [the king]', then he promised to treat them as his kinswomen, to see that they had all necessities for their everyday life and that they should be married to 'gentlemen born' and be given a dowry of £200 per year for life. This promise he made in writing and set to it his sign manual.[30] Part of the arrangements was an annual payment to Elizabeth Woodville, or 'Dame Elizabeth Grey late calling herself Queen of England', of the sum of 700 marks paid quarterly by John Nesfield, squire of the body, who had been in command of the troops watching the sanctuary. This presumably was on condition that she came out of sanctuary, although this was not specified. It has been surmised recently that she lived with her younger daughters in the manor of Heytesbury in Wiltshire, which had been recently granted to Nesfield. This is possible, although the fact that Nesfield was on active service, and was later appointed lieutenant of the tower of Ruysbank at Calais, makes it unlikely that he would have taken a very active part in their supervision.[31] Quite what induced Elizabeth to agree to terms with Richard has been discussed at length. Until recently she had apparently been his bitter enemy – bitter enough to agree to let her eldest daughter marry Henry Tudor, his avowed enemy – and presumably at that time she may have believed that Richard had murdered her two younger sons. Whatever was said to her privately, it had obviously caused her to change her mind. Not only that, but Vergil tells us that she wrote to her eldest son, the Marquess of Dorset, who was then with Tudor in France, and told him to return to England where he would find favour with the king. Dorset apparently tried to take up this offer later, see below p. 47.[32]

On 20 February, the last day of the Parliament, Richard was granted for life the usual tonnage and poundage duties paid by importers of wine and other goods. At the same time Convocation meeting at St Pauls granted him a tax of a Tenth (of the value of their movable goods). At this point it must really have seemed to Richard that his throne was now secure. The situation in the country was indeed as stable now as it would ever be in his reign.

Chapter 2

Preparing for Invasion

Despite his new feeling of security, Richard did not relax. Interestingly one of the steps he took to help defend his realm was to make use of the new technology of firearms, perhaps rather more use than his brother Edward had done. From as early as July 1483 William Nele, a gunner, had been working in the Tower of London and elsewhere making cannon. At the end of December 1483 Richard recruited William Clowke of Gelderland, 'gunmaker', and on 18 January he agreed with one John Bramburgh to make 'certain great stuff of gunpowder'. On 5 March he appointed one Roger Bykeley to 'take' (perhaps commandeer) carpenters and other workmen, cannon and other necessaries, as well as more conventional weapons, for the defence of the realm. Bykeley had already taken delivery (by warrant dated 27 February) of '7 serpentines upon carts, 28 hacbushes with their frames', gunpowder, arrows, bows and bowstrings. (A serpentine was a small-bore weapon, often used at sea, while a hacbush was rather like a rifle, or sometimes a handgun, often called a hackbut.) On 11 March Patrick de la Mote was appointed 'chief cannoner or master founder' of the king's cannon, with two gunners for his attendants. Richard also bought twenty new guns and two serpentines for £24.[1]

In the eight months after the dissolution of his Parliament, Richard spent most of his time away from Westminster, seeking to make his kingdom as secure from invasion as possible. Between 8 March and 9 November he spent only two weeks in Westminster in August.[2] He spent most of his time in Nottingham, from where he probably felt that he could deal with threats to most parts of his kingdom, but he also moved around further north, spending time in York, Middleham, Scarborough and Pontefract, and visiting other places. Thus, on 8 March the king and queen set out from Westminster to make a slow progress to Nottingham. On 9 March they entered Cambridge, where they stayed for two days. During his visit here Richard seems to have made a good impression, and in gratitude for the benefactions of the king and queen the University authorities obtained a decree from the Archbishop of York, Chancellor of the University, who was present during the visit, that a mass be celebrated annually on 2 May 'for the happy state of the same most renowned prince and his dearest consort Anne'.[3] It has been suggested, on the strength of a payment to the 'servants of the Lord Prince', that the Prince of Wales was also in Cambridge at this time, but it seems unlikely that a young child such as Edward would be expected to undertake what was at least an eight-day journey (there and back) from Yorkshire to see his parents for two days, especially in view of the fact that they were apparently on their way to Middleham where he was then living.

After leaving Cambridge, the king and queen travelled slowly to Nottingham, via Huntingdon, Stamford and Grantham. They had arrived at Nottingham by 20 March, on which date several grants were made. Here, some two to three weeks later, probably early in April, and quite without warning, they heard of the sudden death of their only son at Middleham castle. Richard and Anne received this news with great grief. The Crowland Chronicler says, 'You might have seen his father and mother, after hearing the news at Nottingham where they were then staying, almost out of their minds for a long time faced with this sudden grief.' The exact date of the prince's death is unclear. The Crowland Chronicler says it was 'on a day not far off King Edward's anniversary', which would have been 9 April. John Rous states that he died 'an unfortunate death' at Easter time, which was 18 April in 1484. Many authors, unable to resist the suggestion of nemesis overtaking King Richard, have said that his son died on the exact anniversary of the death of Edward IV, whose son he had supplanted. There is a tradition that afterwards Richard called Nottingham the Castle of his Care.[4]

The king and queen stayed in Nottingham for some two weeks after hearing the disastrous news of Edward's death. Richard, probably with

his queen, left on 27 April and went to York, arriving there on 1 May and
staying for three days, although the royal presence was not noticed in the
official council record. It seems possible that this visit to York was made
in order to attend the prince's funeral. There is no record of where
Edward of Middleham was buried but there is a strong possibility that it
was in York Minster, a suitable place for a Prince of Wales, and where
Richard later that year planned and set in hand work for a major chantry
chapel.[5] At about this time the king re-instituted the system of couriers
set up by his brother during the campaign against Scotland in 1482. By
this system, with each courier riding 20 miles and then handing the
message to the next man, news could be sent 200 miles in two days, or
roughly the distance from London to Newcastle.[6] The rumours about
Henry Tudor had started again and by this means Richard hoped to be
able to know as soon as possible when and where any invasion took place.
As another part of his preparations for the defence of the realm Richard
again issued commissions of array to most of the counties of England;
rather poignantly, the name of Edward, Prince of Wales still appeared on
those for the northern counties.[7]

From York Richard went further north to Middleham, where his son
had died, and from here he spent the summer moving around the north,
travelling to Pontefract, Scarborough, York and Durham. He did not
return to Nottingham until the end of July. He spent his time
strengthening his defences. In the north there were several threats, not
least from French ships that were active in the North Sea. Although
Richard prepared ships and men in Scarborough to counter this threat,
the French ships in the area captured several English ships, one of which
was captained by John Nesfield, the king's esquire who had watched over
Elizabeth Woodville while she was in sanctuary. He and his fellow captive
Sir Thomas Everingham were both ransomed by Richard. There was
military action on the Scottish border too, albeit not very effective on
either side, despite the king's decision to dispatch with his expeditionary
force the Duke of Albany, brother of the King of Scots, and the Earl of
Douglas, both long-term pensioners of the English. The Scots were

active at sea too, but here they were thoroughly beaten by a newly refitted English fleet.[8]

Following this rather ineffective military activity in Scotland, Richard made another difficult decision. The death of his only legitimate child left him with no obvious heir, and it was a matter of urgent political necessity that he should make it clear who his new heir would be. It has been suggested that not long after the death of his son he nominated as his heir Edward, Earl of Warwick, son of his elder brother the Duke of Clarence. This is based on the plain statement of John Rous that 'not long after the death of the prince ... the young Earl of Warwick ... was proclaimed heir apparent in the royal court'.[9] According to Rous, Warwick was afterwards arrested and the Earl of Lincoln was given preference. However, it is very unlikely that Richard would have chosen Edward of Warwick as his heir, and there is no evidence other than Rous that he did so. When Warwick's father the Duke of Clarence was attainted he was 'corrupted in blood' and his heirs rendered incapable of inheriting any claim to the throne. Attainders could be reversed and often were, but in this case such a reversal would give the young earl a superior claim to the throne than Richard himself had. For this reason it seem unlikely that Richard would have declared Warwick his heir, and in July he chose as his heir his nephew John de la Pole, Earl of Lincoln, son of his eldest surviving sister Elizabeth, Duchess of Suffolk. That Lincoln was already an adult was an additional bonus. No formal declaration of Lincoln's new role was made, but he was appointed President of the Council of the North, a new institution which in effect seems to have been the council that the Prince of Wales would have controlled. Lincoln was also made Lieutenant of Ireland in August, a dignity that had been held previously by the late Prince of Wales and by previous Yorkist heirs.[10]

At the beginning of August Richard spent nearly three weeks in London, perhaps partly so he could take part on 12 August in the translation of the body of Henry VI from Chertsey Abbey to Windsor. Richard was certainly in Windsor a week later, on his way back to Nottingham.[11] While in London the king took another step towards securing his borders when he sent a safe conduct for Scots ambassadors to come to Nottingham to discuss a truce. The King of Scotland, James III, had been persistently trying to negotiate with Richard for some time, despite the hostile activity along the border and the unpopularity of this policy in Scotland. It must have seemed to Richard at this point that a truce with Scotland would give him one less problem to cope with. He was, in fact, in no position to mount a full-scale campaign against the Scots, given the need to secure the south of England against invasion. On 16 September the Scottish ambassadors entered Nottingham and presented their credentials to the king as he sat in state under a canopy in the great hall of the castle, with his officers around him. Present were the Archbishop of York, the Chancellor, the Bishop of Lincoln and other bishops, John Gunthorp, Keeper of the Privy Seal, the Duke of Norfolk, the Earl of Northumberland and other prominent lords and officials, many of whom would take part in the subsequent negotiations. The commissioners appointed by the king for this task also included Thomas Barow, Master of the Rolls, and Sir William Hussey, Chief Justice of the King's Bench, to add some legal gravitas. The Scots included the Earl of Argyll, Chancellor of Scotland, the Bishop of Aberdeen and two of James's councillors. the Lords Lyle and Oliphant. The men on both sides were thus of considerable rank and, perhaps importantly in terms of diplomacy, of roughly equal status. After the presentation of the credentials, Archibald Whitelaw, James III's secretary, gave a very flowery speech praising the abilities, appearance and intentions of King Richard. The negotiations must have gone well because by 21 September a three-year truce between the two countries had been agreed; on the same day a marriage was also arranged between James, Duke of Rothesay, James III's heir, and Anne de la Pole, sister of Richard's heir the Earl of Lincoln.[12] This marriage never took place. Anne de la Pole did not marry and later entered a convent, while the Duke of Rothesay (as James IV) married Margaret Tudor, the eldest daughter of Henry VII.

During the summer there had also been a small-scale sea war against the Bretons, and as part of his plans to settle foreign problems, it was in Richard's interest to come to terms with Brittany, the last independent province in France. Brittany needed support to counter unfriendly French intentions, and it must have been clear to Richard that an alliance with Brittany would give him a lever to use against France if necessary – and also against Henry Tudor and his ever-growing band of exiles living there. Much diplomatic activity took place and in June a truce was signed with Francis, Duke of Brittany, to last from 1 July 1483 to 24 April 1485.[13] A letter was sent on 17 June directed to the sheriffs of various southern counties requiring them to issue a proclamation announcing the dates of this truce, presumably directed at seamen who might violate it. The duke himself was ill and the correspondence was carried on by his minister, Pierre Landois. As part of the agreement the English promised to provide 1,000 archers to help the Bretons maintain their borders against the French, and the English commitment to this went as far as the appointment on 6 June of commissioners led by Francis, Lord Lovell to muster the archers at Southampton; on 26 June a captain (John Grey, Lord Powis) was placed in command of them. However, this force seems never to have set sail.[14] As part of the treaty the English almost certainly insisted that Duke Francis cease to support Henry Tudor. Landois apparently agreed to this, and promised either to keep Henry and his leading supporters in protective custody or even to hand them over to Richard. The negotiations with Brittany seem to have gone on over the summer, and William Catesby, Richard's Chancellor of the Exchequer and an influential councillor, was in Brittany in September 1484 when he made an offering in Vannes cathedral.

The negotiations may also have included an offer to restore to Duke Francis the revenues from the lands of the earldom of Richmond, coincidentally the earldom to which Tudor laid claim and which had been held by the Dukes of Brittany in the fourteenth century. Richard also promised to give the duke the lands of the other English exiles if he agreed to keep Tudor and his associates in close custody. At some point in the late summer of 1484 the mercenary Juan de Salazar was dispatched to talk to King Richard. It is not clear who sent him: it may have been Duke Francis of Brittany, but may also have been Maximilian, King of the Romans, whose mercenary captain Salazar was and for whom he had fought in Flanders. Salazar probably left England in early September but he plays a further part in English history, as will be seen.[15]

Fortunately for Henry, but not for Richard, these elaborate plans came to the notice of John Morton, Bishop of Ely, who was then in Flanders, having fled there after the failure of the Buckingham uprising. Morton may have heard it from the Countess of Richmond, Henry's mother, and she perhaps from her husband Lord Stanley, who was a member of Richard's council. Morton sent Sir Christopher Urswick, an associate of the Countess of Richmond, to warn Tudor. The dates of these events are confused but Tudor seems to have been warned of his imminent arrest by the Bretons at some time in late September; by elaborate means Henry fled from Vannes, the capital of Brittany, with a few companions, arriving over the border in France just in time to avoid the troops sent after him by Landois. The great numbers of exiles whom Tudor had left behind were allowed by the duke to leave Brittany and join Tudor in France, where Charles VIII, the King of France, allowed them to remain. Richard had gained nothing by his initiative and Henry Tudor was now in the hands of a much greater power than Brittany, and one that might gain diplomatic advantage by supporting the earl. As it turned out, it did suit the French to help the exiles, since until the time Tudor set sail for England again in the summer of 1485, they were concerned to keep England busy thinking of invasion in order to prevent her helping Brittany in a military capacity. Just days after Tudor's ships set sail, the French signed a peace treaty with Duke Francis and thereafter no longer needed to worry about Brittany. As Charles Ross puts it: 'One week later and the Tudor dynasty might never have been born.'[16]

Not long after Tudor escaped to France, he was joined at his headquarters in Angers by the Earl of Oxford, a veteran Lancastrian commander and a very experienced soldier. Oxford had been in prison in Hammes castle, in the pale of Calais, since 1474, but he managed to escape from Hammes in December 1484, together with James Blount, the castle's commander, and John Fortescue, the gentleman porter of the castle. This was a serious blow to Richard, as the stability of his entire realm could easily be threatened by events in Calais. The garrison at Calais was the only standing body of troops in England, and it had played a pivotal part in the wars of the recent past, notably when in the hands of the Earl of Warwick, who had been Captain of Calais back in 1471. In 1483 Richard had executed the present Captain of Calais, Lord Hastings, with no reaction from the garrison, and Lord Dynham, Hastings' deputy, remained in charge. Richard had already realised that with Henry Tudor at large in France, the Earl of Oxford should be removed from Calais and brought back to England before he could find a way to join Tudor, and he duly sent a warrant from Nottingham ordering Blount to convey Oxford to the French coast and hence to England. But Oxford had apparently already suborned Blount, and both fled to join Tudor. Dynham, who remained loyal to Richard, reacted quickly to the news of the events at Hammes and besieged the castle with his Calais troops, presumably in an attempt to prevent any more defections. Richard offered pardons to the Hammes troops on 16 and 30 November, and separately to Blount on the same days. The pardon was repeated on 16 January and this time included Blount's wife, who had remained in the castle. The garrison of Guisnes, the other outlying castle in the pale of Calais, was replaced later and Sir James Tyrell, a reliable ally of the king, was put in charge. Dynham was later replaced by Richard's illegitimate son John as Lieutenant of Calais, although this change of command probably never took place.[17] This episode may have seemed to Richard to have more or less restored the status quo, and indeed he had no more problems in Calais, but with hindsight it is obvious that it was another indication of how fragile was the loyalty to his regime.

By November 1484 the threat of an invasion that year had receded and Richard returned to London on 10 November, although he did not settle there until 28 November, first touring Kent, perhaps to check that everything possible had been done there to calm this previously restless county. Once in London he could reflect on what had been accomplished in the year; the treaties with Brittany and Scotland were not perfect but they had served to pacify at least some of his enemies. He had not managed to neutralise Henry Tudor but there was the hope that if France did not actively support Tudor for a year or two, then Richard would have time to consolidate his power so that he would be strong enough to fight off any possible invasion by Tudor. To make sure, as far as possible, that

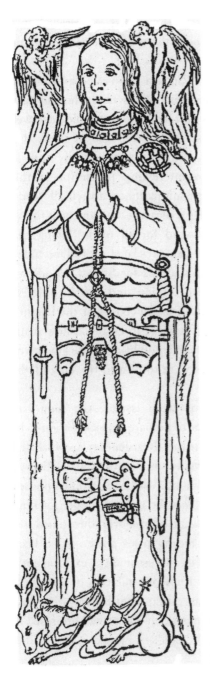

The alabaster effigy of the Earl of Oxford, d. 1514, formerly in Colne Priory but now lost. (*Geoffrey Wheeler*)

his forces would be ready for when they were needed, he reissued on 8 December the commissions of array, mostly to the men he had appointed before.

As well as the commissions of array, Richard also issued guidance to the commissioners, asking them to check that all the men who had been promised previously were still available and that they were able men, well horsed and harnessed, and 'no rascals'. They were also to check that money set aside for the purpose was still held appropriately and, in effect, had not been embezzled. An interesting postscript to this exhortation was an instruction for the commissioners to tell all 'lords, nobles, captains and others' that the king's pleasure was for them to put aside all private grudges and quarrels and for all to be 'loving and assisting to other in the king's quarrels'. Ten days later, on 18 December, another message was sent to the commissioners for Surrey, Middlesex and Hertfordshire – the counties nearest London, and therefore able to respond fastest – asking them, in effect, to take a census of the knights, squires and gentlemen in their respective areas to establish how many men, 'defensibly arrayed', each one of them could bring to the king given half a day's notice. The commissioners were to inform the king of the totals as soon as possible.[18]

Not long before these commissions were issued, the king had instructed the Chancellor on 7 December to prepare a proclamation to be sent to the sheriffs. This was written in the Ricardian style, which has been described as 'spirited' – and it certainly is that. It is as if Richard believed that his opponents must be immoral just because they opposed him, he being conscious that his cause was the righteous one; for him, governing the realm was a moral crusade and anyone who threatened this crusade must be struck down by every means in his power. It has been plausibly argued that this document and its successor are so extravagantly worded that it would be impossible for Richard's subjects to take them seriously. This may well have been the case, although it cleverly played on English patriotism and chauvinism in saying that Tudor had promised to give up all claim to the French throne and lands in France.

The proclamation begins:

Forasmuch as the king our sovereign lord hath certain knowledge that Piers, Bishop of Exeter, Thomas Grey, late Marquis Dorset, Jasper late Earl of Pembroke, John late Earl of Oxenford and Sir Edward Wodevylle with others divers his rebels and traitors, disabled and attainted by the authority of the High Court of Parliament, of whom many be known for open murderers and adulterers and extortioners, contrary to the pleasure of God and against all truth honour and nature hath forsaken their natural country taking them first to be under the obeisance of the Duke of Bretayn and to him promised certain things which by him and his council were thought things to be greatly unnatural for them to grant ... [and who therefore refused to help] ... They seeing that the said duke and his council would not aid nor succour them nor follow their ways privily departed out of his country into France and there taking them to be under the obeisance of the king's ancient enemy Charles calling himself King of France and ... the said rebels and traitors have chosen to be their captain one Harry late calling himself Earl of Richmond which of his ambitious and insatiable covetousness encroaches and usurped upon him the name and title of royal estate of this realm of England whereunto he hath no manner interest, right, title or colour as every man well knoweth.

Not only this, but Tudor had agreed to give up all claims of the kings of England to the 'crown and realm of France, together with the duchies of Normandy, Gascony and Guienne', as well as all of the Calais lands and castles. The proclamation continued in this vein, warning that if Tudor and his adherents won they would subvert the laws and confiscate the property of all subjects, and 'do the most cruel murders, slaughters and robberies and disinheritances that ever were seen in any Christian realm'. The king promised 'as a well willed, diligent and courageous prince' to 'put his most royal person to all labour and pain necessary in this behalf for the resistance and subduing of his said enemies' and asked his subjects to do the same.[19] An almost identical proclamation was issued in June 1485, but this time omitting Dorset. Richard could for the moment do no more to defend his realm and allowed himself to celebrate Christmas.

That this proclamation was necessary is shown by the letter sent to the Mayor of Windsor (and very probably to other towns) on 6 December, stating that a number of false reports were circulating, 'and for as much as we be credibly informed that our rebels and traitors, now confedered with our ancient enemies of France by many and sundry ways conspire and study the means to the subversion of this our realm and of unity amongst our subjects as in tending writings, by seditious persons with counterfeit and contrive false inventions, tidings and rumours to the intent to provoke and stir discord betwixt us and our lords', it then goes on to command that 'if any such rumours or writings come amongst you to search and enquire of the first shewers and utterers thereof and when that you shall so find ye do commit unto sure ward and after proceed to their sharp punishment in example and fear of all other'.[20] It has been suggested that an undated message from Henry Tudor was one of the 'writings' referred to in Richard's letter. It is addressed to Henry's 'Right trusty and honourable friends and our allies', and it reads:

I greet you well. Being given to understand your good devoir and intent to advance me to the furtherance of my rightful claim due and lineal inheritance of the crown and for the just depriving of that homicide and unnatural tyrant which now unjustly bears dominion over you, I give you to understand that no Christian heart can be more full of joy and gladness than the heart of me your poor exiled friend who will upon the instance of your sure advertise what powers you will make ready and what captains and leaders you get to conduct be prepared to pass over the sea with such forces as my friends here are preparing for me. And if I have such good speed and success as I wish according to your desire I shall ever be most forward to remember, and wholly to requite this your most loving kindness in my just quarrel. Given under our signet, H.

I pray you give credence to the messenger of what he shall impart to you.

This missive was signed as though Henry were already king (he used an elaborate H as his sign manual after he took the throne) and is written in a rather sycophantic manner. It certainly had the result, deliberately or not, of annoying Richard, the actual king.[21]

One event in particular shows the seriousness with which cases of treasonous correspondence were treated. This concerned William Colingbourne, who posted a rhyme on the door of St Paul's Cathedral in London reading, 'The cat, the rat and Lovel our dog, Ruleth all England under a Hog', the names referring to Richard (as the hog) and to his chief advisers Lord Lovell, William Catesby and Sir Richard Ratcliff. For this, Shakespeare tells us Colingbourne was hanged, drawn and quartered. He was certainly condemned to this punishment but not because of the rhyme; in fact he had been in correspondence with Tudor. A powerful commission of inquiry was appointed on 29 November 1484, its terms of reference being to investigate 'certain treasons and offences committed by William Colyngbourne, late of Lydyard, co. Wilts, esquire and John Turbervyle late of Fyremayne, co. Dorset, esquire'. The commissioners included the Dukes of Norfolk and Suffolk, the Earl of Surrey (son of the Duke of Norfolk), Lord Lovell, eleven other lords, the Lord Mayor of London and nine ordinary judges, so there can be no doubt how seriously the offence was viewed. According to Holinshed, who apparently quoted the original indictment (which no longer exists), Colingbourne and Turberville had paid someone £8 to take a letter to Tudor encouraging him to invade England again in the autumn, telling him to land at Poole and offering to meet him there with a powerful force. As an extra inducement, they promised him that if he took power at that time he would be able to collect the revenues payable in the realm at Michaelmas.[22]

Richard's Christmas season was apparently celebrated with particular magnificence, perhaps to emphasise his confidence in the state of his realm. It was held at Westminster and on Epiphany (6 January) the king wore his crown and took a full part in the ceremonies in the great hall there 'as though at his original coronation'. Christmas itself was also well celebrated, with the Crowland Chronicler disapprovingly remarking that 'too much attention was paid to singing and dancing and to vain changes of clothing of identical shape and colour given to both Queen Anne and Lady Elizabeth, eldest daughter of the dead king'.[23] The significance of this statement is debatable, but it sounds as if all present (except perhaps the Chronicler) enjoyed themselves.

During the Christmas festivities Richard's spies reported to him that in the coming year there would certainly be an invasion by Henry Tudor, who, by the favour of Charles VIII of France, was busy fitting out ships and gathering men in France.[24] To repel any invasion, Richard was going to need money. The men he would call out when the time came would be paid for by the individuals or towns bringing or sending them, but he would need money for his ships and garrisons – the sinews of war, to use a modern phrase. Probably reluctantly, he decided to raise the money by means of loans. He must have known this would be an unpopular move, as his brother Edward had often raised money by means of 'Benevolences' – semi-forced 'gifts' to the king – that were rarely repaid, and Richard's Parliament had passed an act forbidding them. Richard's system was different because he issued the requests under the privy seal and bound the crown to repay them at specified dates. The letters he sent out were baldly headed in the Privy Seal register 'A letter for money' and went on:

By the king

Trusty and welbeloved we greet you well. And for such great and excessive costs and charges as we hastily must bear and sustain as well for the keeping of the sea as otherwise for the defence of this Realm we desire and in our heartiest wise pray you to send unto us by way of loan by our trusty servant this bearer. And we promise you by these our letter signed with our own [hand] truly to content you thereof at Martinmas next coming and residue at the feast [of] Saint John Baptist then next following without further delay. Assuring you that accomplishing this our instant desire and hearty prayer you shall find us your good and gracious sovereign lord in any your reasonable desires hereafter giving further credence to our said servant in such thing as shall open unto you on our behalf touching this matter. Given etc.

These letters were sent out in bundles, carried by bearers with instructions to give them to named recipients, who were scattered around most of England. The bearers were enjoined to ask them for the sums 'written within the corner and end' of some of the letters. The amounts varied between £100 and 40 marks. Others had no names written in but contained an amount to be asked for, and were to be given to people at the bearers' discretion.

Another letter was sent to those being asked for the money. This letter was similar to that above, although couched in rather more pressing terms. As well as saying that the money was needed for the defence of the realm and the surety of the king's royal person, it further said that the king and 'all his lords' were 'thinking that every true Englishman will help him in this behalf of which number his Grace reputes and takes you for one'. The whole system was amazingly well organised and lists of those who were to receive named letters and blank letters, together with the names of the bearers, are preserved in the register of the Privy Seal writs. The bearers of the letters were obviously thought to be particularly trustworthy (they included Thomas Lynom, the King's Solicitor General, and John Kendall, his secretary). The total amount asked for has been calculated to be in the order of £30,000. We cannot be sure how much was actually raised, of course, because we do not know how many of the unnamed letters were actually handed out, nor can we know how many people actually complied, but it was an extraordinary effort. We do not know if Richard would have repaid the money, although given his general character it seems probable that he would at least have tried to. Unfortunately he was dead before the first repayment date fell due and we have no evidence that Henry VII repaid the money.[25]

These letters were sent out over a period of six weeks, between 21 February and 5 April. By the time the last ones were being delivered, Queen Anne was dead. She was apparently taken ill very soon after Christmas and took to her bed, which the doctors had forbidden Richard to share. This is usually interpreted nowadays to indicate that she was suffering from tuberculosis, as this was the standard response to this disease at the time. She died on 16 March, at the time of an eclipse of the sun, and was buried in Westminster Abbey with great honours.[26] Later chroniclers imply – or state – that the queen's illness and death were partly due to Richard spurning her and because he had commented openly that he wanted to be rid of her in order to marry his niece Elizabeth.[27]

There was certainly a rumour that Richard intended to marry his niece, but it seems unlikely that it started as early as Christmas, as the Crowland Chronicler says.[28] However, it was certainly in circulation soon after the death of the queen, and Richard was forced to deal with it. It seems unlikely that he would ever have seriously considered such a thing. To marry Elizabeth would be to ignore the fact that she, and her brothers, had been declared illegitimate, and such a move would call into question Richard's own claim to the throne, which was based on their illegitimacy. We are told that two leading councillors, Sir Richard Ratcliffe and William Catesby (recently Speaker of Parliament), argued strongly against the possibility on the grounds that people in the north would not stand for it. They held the memory of Queen Anne very dear, they said, not least because she was the younger daughter of the Earl of Warwick, who had been very popular in the north. Richard was also told that the Pope would not offer a dispensation from the decrees forbidding marriage with such close relatives. This was not strictly true, but such marriages were certainly not known in England. The final argument (probably unspoken) was that if Elizabeth ever became queen, she might seek revenge against those who had been responsible for the deaths of her uncle Earl Rivers and her half-brother Richard Grey.

Whatever the truth of it, shortly before Easter, probably on 30 March, Richard decided to put a stop to the rumour. He gathered the mayor, councillors and chief citizens of the city of London in the great hall of the Order of St John at Clerkenwell, and denied 'in a loud clear voice' that he had ever considered marrying his niece. He also denounced rumour-mongering in general.[29] Nothing is known of the feelings of the Princess Elizabeth about this matter, although it is possible that she may have desired such a marriage. In a letter said to have been in the Howard archives in the late sixteenth century (although not seen since), and written to John Howard, Duke of Norfolk, Elizabeth asks the duke to be her mediator 'as before' in the 'cause of her marriage to the king, who as she wrote was her only joy and maker in this world and that she was his in heart and thoughts, in body and in all'. She went on to say that she feared that the Queen [Anne] would never die. This letter was apparently written in the middle of February 1485. It was an extraordinary letter, and if the text as we have it is an accurate paraphrase, then there is no doubt that Elizabeth wanted to marry the king. If this were so, then presumably she did not believe that he had murdered her brothers. However, we do not have the full text, and it has been argued that a slight change of punctuation would make the text mean that Elizabeth wanted the king to advance her marriage to the Duke of Beja (see below); the fact remains that since we do not have the original, we may never know what is meant, no matter what we do with the punctuation in the version we have.[30]

To suppress these rumours and counter-rumours, which had apparently spread around the country again (as they had in late 1483), the king sent a letter to York and probably to other towns too. It was couched in similar terms to his denunciation of the rumours in London at St John's. The letter described the lies, rumours and slanders that were being spread across the realm about the king and his officers as trying to 'avert' people's minds from the king, 'sending forth of false and abominable language' and by other means whereby innocent people could put themselves into danger by following this false information. He told the York men that he had lately called before him the mayor and aldermen of the city of London, together with citizens and the Lords Spiritual and Temporal, as well as his household, 'to whom we largely showed our true intent and mind in all such things as the said noise and disclaunder [slander]'. He did not mention the chief rumour about Princess Elizabeth that he had so vigorously denied. He went on to say that he had charged the London authorities to check all such slander and lies, to arrest the persons guilty and punish them and to be vigilant against such things. He further charged the mayor and council of York to do the same, as they 'will eschew our grievous indignation and answer unto us at your extreme peril'.[31]

However, the rumour that Richard was to marry again was at least partly based in truth, and that he was not averse to doing so despite the recent death of his wife is shown by the negotiations that went on during the spring and summer of 1485 in Portugal, where Edward Brampton, Richard's envoy, was delicately asking for the hand of Princess Joanna, sister of John II of Portugal. Brampton left England not long after the death of Queen Anne, which suggests some rather indecent haste on Richard's part to remarry, but in the light of his own need to remarry, and his obligation to organise a marriage for Elizabeth, such unseemly haste may perhaps be excused because Brampton was also proposing that Princess Elizabeth should marry Manuel, Duke of Beja, cousin of John II and later King Manuel I. At a stroke this would have destroyed Henry Tudor's plans to marry Elizabeth in order to unite the warring houses of York and Lancaster, and would have given Richard a claim to be doing the same thing since Joanna was a member of the senior legitimate Lancastrian line after the extinction of the line from Henry IV. Joanna had received many proposals of marriage but had rejected them all in favour of a religious life, but there is evidence that she was prepared to accept Richard's offer. Negotiations were only broken off when news of the death of Richard at Bosworth reached Portugal.[32] It may perhaps be useful to say that if the King of Portugal was prepared to see his sister married to Richard III, then he presumably did not regard him as a villain.

At this moment in his reign, Richard seemed more than ever to be trying to impose on his people his vision of how things should be, morally and in justice. In the grant of the Principality of Wales to his son, he had described it as a 'vocation to which we are called by God's favour to govern and be set at the head of all the mortals of this realm', which was not a common phrase in such grants.[33] All of his proclamations similarly have a moral dimension, as though he were trying to persuade his subjects into a better way of life and to show them that he was determined to see that they would receive justice. It sometimes appeared that he was personally affronted by immorality and felt that he must do something about it, and that anyone who threatened this ideal must be dealt with, as, for example, in his proclamation against Henry Tudor and his allies. Interestingly the next item in the Privy Seal register after that proclamation was another in which the king said 'that for the love that he hath for the ministration and execution of justice' he promised that if anyone found themselves unjustly accused in any way, they should tell the king and according to justice and his laws they should have remedy. In mid–March 1485 he issued a proclamation to each bishop in his realm assuring them that in the midst of his many cares and business, his 'principal intent and desire is to see virtue and cleanness of living to be advanced, increased and multiplied and vices and all other things repugnant to virtue provoking the high indignation and fearful displeasure of God to be repressed and annulled'. He assured the bishops that he would support them in their endeavours to work towards this ideal and to see that all who 'set apart virtue and promote the damnable execution of sin and vices' should be reformed or punished.[34]

Anne's death must have been a grievous blow for the embattled king, but perhaps not as grievous as might have been thought in the light of the above. Even so, he had to recover quickly because it had become obvious that Tudor's invasion was going to happen that year. News had come that Tudor had obtained promises of support from Charles VIII, King of France and was fitting out an invasion fleet in Harfleur. At about this time, or perhaps a little later, the Marquess of Dorset, Elizabeth Woodville's eldest son, took up the offer probably made to him in the winter of 1484 of returning to England, and tried to flee from France. He was stopped beyond Compiegne, just before he could cross the French border, by Humphrey Cheney and Matthew Baker, two of Tudor's men whom Tudor, with the permission of the French government, had sent in pursuit. Dorset was persuaded to return to Tudor. One wonders what form the persuasion took; certainly Dorset's desertion would have been disastrous for Tudor in political terms and because he had knowledge of all his plans.[35] It seems likely that Dorset's flight took place at about this time, or perhaps a little later, because the proclamation against the rebels issued in December 1484 condemns him, while that issued in June 1485 does not; perhaps even this late in the day Richard still hoped that Dorset would leave Tudor. This omission of Dorset's name from the June proclamation might have been part of a wider strategy; on 11 December 1484 John Morton, Bishop of Ely was granted a general pardon, as was Richard Woodville, the brother of Queen Elizabeth, on 30 March 1485. We know that neither of these two rebels took up their pardons, but Richard must have considered it worth trying to detach them from Tudor.[36]

The rumour that Richard was planning to marry Elizabeth of York was enough to 'pinch Henry to the very stomach', to quote Vergil. It may well have caused him anxiety, for not only would such a union have spoilt his plans to unite the red rose with the white, but it might also have caused those Yorkists in his party who did not support Richard III to desert Tudor. In response, Henry and his advisers came up with the idea for Henry to marry instead the sister of Walter Herbert, second son of Tudor's former guardian Walter Herbert, Earl of Pembroke, using as an intermediary the Earl of Northumberland, who was married to Maud, the daughter of the Earl of Pembroke. Tudor was presumably therefore in contact with Northumberland, although this plan seems not to have been even presented to Herbert. Herbert's eldest son the Earl of Huntingdon was married to Richard's illegitimate daughter Katherine, and was thus the king's son-in-law, so it is interesting to speculate about the result of these negotiations had they gone ahead. Of course, Richard could have thwarted Tudor's marriage plans by the simple of expedient of marrying Elizabeth to a suitable gentleman; he did not need to marry her himself. Perhaps the Portuguese negotiations with the Duke of Beja were part of just such a plan.[37]

Since his arrival in France in late September 1484 Henry Tudor had been trying to persuade the government of Charles VIII to support him. In November Charles granted Henry some money to clothe the several hundred men he had with him and allowed him to recruit mercenaries, although it isn't clear what he was to pay them with. Late in the year on 20 December there started a series of events that seem to have concentrated the minds of the French government and perhaps made them think that now was the time to give Tudor some proper aid to help him invade England. The series of events began with a high-ranking embassy, led by the Bishop of St Pol de Leon, which the Duke of Brittany commissioned to go to England. This probably arrived after Christmas, when Richard issued power to the Bishop of Lincoln, the Lord Chancellor, John Gunthorp, Dean of Wells and Keeper of the Privy Seal, and four others to discuss the extension of the truce with Brittany. The seniority of the men involved indicates how important the occasion was thought to be on both sides, and only two weeks later Richard announced that the truce had been extended until 1492 – a length of truce unknown for very many years.[38] This virtual peace treaty between his two enemies, Brittany and England, seems to have galvanised Charles VIII into action and he agreed to help Tudor, not least to distract England. At Rouen in May Charles requested aid from the regional estates assembled there to help Henry recover the realm to which, Charles assured the assembly, he had a better right than anyone else. The aid was duly granted and preliminary preparations towards assembling a fleet were begun at the mouth of the river Seine. As summer progressed, the preparation of the ships, which were provided by the French, and the assembling of men went on apace. Charles gave Henry a grant of 40,000 livres and loaned him more. He also gave him a few pieces of artillery. To pay for his troops, Henry also borrowed money from French merchants. It is not clear how many men Henry had raised, but traditionally he left France with about 4,000 men in all (see below for a discussion on the size of Tudor's army). Some of them, about 1,800 in all, were discharged soldiers from the French military base at Pont de l'Arche, which had recently closed down. These men were trained soldiers and would form the core of the invading army. Another group, recruited at the last minute, may be those whom Philip de Commines, the Burgundian chronicler and diplomat, said were 'as bad as could have been found anywhere'. It has been pointed out that the closing down of the base at Pont l'Arche, and the subsequent discharge of all of the men there, would very likely result in ex-soldiers wandering about in Normandy and perhaps looking for a new cause, so that all the French troops recruited by Tudor may have come from Pont l'Arche. The French soldiers were commanded by Philibert de Chandée, probably a member of the house of Savoy. Charles also allowed a group of Scots then serving in his armies to join Tudor. They were commanded by Alexander Bruce of Earlshall, Captain of the Scots Horse, John of Haddington and Henderson of Haddington, Captain of the Scots Foot. Bruce was later rewarded by Tudor with an annuity of £20. In addition to the Scots, there were an unknown number of exiles who had gathered round Tudor, perhaps as many as 400 of them. These included his uncle Jasper Tudor and the Earl of Oxford, both experienced soldiers. Leaving behind Marquess Dorset and John Bourchier as pledges for the repayment of the loans, a fleet of perhaps twenty ships (Tudor had fifteen ships for about 2,000 men in 1483) sailed from the Seine on 1 August. The fleet was commanded by Guillaume de Casenove, nicknamed Coulon.[39]

From this point Richard concentrated all his efforts directly on the defence of the realm. Sir George Neville, son of Lord Abergavenny (a cousin of the king), commanded a small fleet, presumably in the Channel, while Richard's Chamberlain, Viscount Lovell, another strong supporter, was based near Southampton, perhaps at Plymouth, with another fleet, with instructions to watch all neighbouring ports and to repel invasion.[40] This was the best point to watch for Tudor's invasion fleet since he was known to be fitting out in the Seine. As far as we know, the Duke of Norfolk, another staunch supporter of the king, was on his estates in East Anglia and could be relied on to guard that coast and the approaches to London. There was no chance that Tudor would attempt to land in the north-east, where Richard had widespread support, and it was unlikely he would head for Devon and Cornwall, where he himself had little support. That left Wales as perhaps the most likely point for Tudor to try to reach, especially since he had grown up in Pembroke and his uncle Jasper had formerly been Earl of Pembroke. Nothing had yet formally replaced the enormous power wielded by Buckingham in the whole of Wales, and Richard had made only piecemeal arrangements for the control of the Principality. James Tyrell, his reliable Knight of the Body, had been put in charge of Glamorgan and Morgannock, but he was now ruling through deputies after having been also put in charge of Guisnes castle. The substantial local landowner Rhys ap Thomas had refused to support the

Duke of Buckingham in 1483; although previously a Lancastrian, Richard must have hoped he was now a Yorkist supporter since he had received an annuity from the king. Morgan Kidwelly, the attorney-general, also had influence in Wales. The Chief Justice of South Wales was William Herbert, Earl of Huntingdon, who was married to Richard's illegitimate daughter Katherine. The Herberts had previously been a formidable power in Wales, but the earl himself was not a very effective man, although the king could rely on his brother Walter Herbert. The men of North Wales had been ordered on 13 January 1485 to put themselves at the disposal of Lord Stanley and his brother Sir William, Justice of North Wales, against the rebels. The Stanleys, together with Lord Stanley's son Lord Strange, were powerful in North Wales, Lancashire and Cheshire. Given the somewhat equivocal position the Stanleys had adopted in the past few years, and the fact that Lord Stanley was married to Tudor's mother, this was a high-risk strategy which, unfortunately for Richard, failed. In Wales and other places beacons were placed on hills in order to give speedy warning of invasion.[41] Up to this point Richard had spent most of the last five months in London. On 12 May he went to Windsor and from there he went to Kenilworth and Coventry, and then on to Nottingham, arriving on 12 June. Here, at a central point of the country, he was ideally placed to deal with an invasion at any point on his coasts.

On 22 June he sent letters to the sheriffs of the shires and to his commissioners of array instructing them to take steps to be ready to defend the realm against all rebels and traitors. The wording makes it sound as though an invasion could be expected at any moment: 'And for as much as certain information is made unto us that our rebels and traitors associate with our ancient enemies of France and other strangers intend hastily to invade this our realm'. The letters go on to command that 'with due diligence' they put their commissions into operation in haste. A letter sent at the same time ordered the commissioners to see that all their men were prepared, likewise all knights, squires and gentlemen in their area, all of them to be ready within an hour's warning when commanded. Rather plaintively, it also says that all lords, noble men and so on should set aside their quarrels in order that they should be able to assist the king.

Richard probably said this more in hope than because he thought all men would act so. The sheriffs or their deputies were further ordered to remain within their respective shire towns in order that they might be found easily.[42] The letter to the sheriff of the county of York was received in the city on 8 July, and the council ordered the craft guilds to see that their members were ready to be defensibly arrayed to defend the city.[43]

On 9 July Richard reissued the proclamation he had first issued in December, again under the Great Seal. One of the extant copies went to the Sheriff of Kent, although no copy is recorded as having been received in York. This time the proclamation omitted Marquess Dorset, perhaps because Richard still hoped he might desert Tudor, and in it Henry Tudor was described as 'son of Edmund Tydder, son of Owen Tydder', and it was added for good measure that 'he is descended of bastard blood both of mother side and of father side for the said Owen the grandfather was bastard born and his mother [is descended from] … Dame Katherine Swinford and of her double adultery begotten'. Interestingly Richard casts no doubt on the marriage of Owen Tudor and Katherine de Valois, former queen of Henry V.[44]

Matters were now moving faster. On 24 July Richard sent for the Great Seal, as he needed it to be close at hand so that there would be no delay in issuing instruments under the seal. The message was received by Chancellor John Russell, Bishop of Lincoln, on 29 July. Russell was ordered to hand the seal to Thomas Barowe, Master of the Rolls, and this was duly done on Friday, 29 July 'at the eighth hour … at the Old Temple in the lower oratory … enclosed in a white leather bag sealed with the Chancellor's eagle signet'. Barowe took three days to travel to Nottingham and he delivered the seal to the king in his oratory at about seven in the evening, in the presence of the Archbishop of York, John, Earl of Lincoln, Lord Scrope of Upsall, Lord Strange (eldest son of Lord Stanley) and John Kendall, the king's secretary. Richard then returned the seal to Thomas Barowe to use, appointing him Keeper of the Great Seal. It is sometimes said that Richard's action in asking for the Great Seal effectively dismissed Russell as Lord Chancellor, but it may be that his appointment of Barowe as its Keeper made him a sort of vice-Chancellor, with powers to act in the absence of the Chancellor.[45] Not a great deal was done officially after this, although the Patent Rolls show that a certain amount of routine administration went on up to about 9 August, and there are Exchequer writs in existence that were prepared in the summer of 1485 and altered after Henry became king. On these documents the name Richard has been erased and replaced by Henry, and there are other similar changes. Administrative work was obviously continuing behind the scenes.[46] The king spent a few days in mid-August at his hunting lodge at Beskwood (now Bestwood) near Nottingham, and it was here on 11 August that he received the news of Henry Tudor's landing at Milford Haven in Wales on Sunday, 7 August.

Chapter 3

The Invasion

Tudor sailed from France on 1 August and landed six days later, on 7 August, in the south-west corner of Wales. As noted above, since Tudor was part-Welsh it had certainly occurred to Richard that he would try to make landfall in this area, where he might expect to find friendly faces. In addition, of course, Tudor's uncle Jasper had been Earl of Pembroke and probably still had contacts there. Richard had already made plans to counter an invasion here, but once Tudor had landed the whole situation changed. It was easy enough to swear not to allow Tudor to pass when it seemed he was unlikely to be there in the first place. His physical presence, backed by an army, resulted in some rapid rethinking by the gentry of the area.

Earlier, perhaps in the spring, Tudor had received a message from John Morgan, a Welsh lawyer, to the effect that Sir John Savage (Lord Stanley's nephew) and the influential landowner Rhys ap Thomas, previously mentioned as apparently a supporter of Richard, were both committed to his cause. A copy of the message that Tudor sent to his supporters is known to have been in the ap Thomas papers until it was burnt with the rest in a later fire. Perhaps the letter was sent to ap Thomas when Tudor learnt that he was committed to his cause. Such information would doubtless have strengthened his inclination to land in Wales.[1]

Tudor landed at sunset. He probably came ashore in the small Mill Bay, on the tip of St Anne's Head, just inside the eastern edge of Milford Haven. When he landed, Tudor knelt 'and holding his hands toward heaven meekly and devoutly said these words, *judica me deus et discerne causam meum*.[2] Vergil does not say where exactly he landed but says that he first took a place called 'Dalley'. The small castle at Dale is a short distance from Mill Bay, and when Tudor left his landing place at daybreak the next morning it would have been the first place he came to. He would not have landed at Dale itself, however, as the beach there was overlooked by the castle. Before marching away from his landing place, Tudor knighted some of his companions, including his French commander Philibert de Chandée, his uncle John Welles, now recognised as Lord Welles despite the attainder of 1484, Edward Courtenay, later created Earl of Devon and his 1484 attainder reversed, and John Cheyne, who was traditionally said to have been killed by Richard at Bosworth.[3]

'Nangle', the place where Richard announced that Tudor had landed, is now known as Angle and lies on the other side of Milford Haven from Mill Bay. It has been suggested that Tudor landed some troops there, who marched towards Pembroke, held for Richard by the constable, Richard Williams. This seems unlikely, and it is much more plausible that the news reached Pembroke castle by means of a beacon light on St Anne's Head. Williams may well have told Richard that Tudor's forces had all landed at Angle and believed that they had done so, but he would not necessarily have known the exact landing place.[4]

Henry Tudor's landing was unopposed, and it seems probable that the site had been carefully chosen because it would provide a good landing place and an opportunity to gather his troops together without opposition. The area was controlled by Richard Williams, who had authority over an extensive area of Pembrokeshire; other supporters of Richard controlled other parts of South Wales and the marches, but they all seem to have been taken unawares. From Dale, Tudor marched to Haverfordwest, apparently moving so quickly that he was spoken of only just before he arrived. He may perhaps have blocked the road out of Dale to make sure no information about his arrival went ahead of him. In Haverfordwest he was received peaceably and those who remembered his uncle Jasper as the Earl of Pembroke declared their allegiance through Arnold Butler, a gentleman of Glamorgan.

At Haverfordwest Tudor heard a rumour that Rhys ap Thomas and John Savage were determined to help the king, which undoubtedly caused considerable nervousness in the rebel ranks. Tudor departed from

Haverfordwest on the same day he had arrived, perhaps in case the rumour was true, and marched north towards Cardigan. This route would take him away from the strongly Ricardian South Wales and towards North Wales, where he doubtless hoped to pick up additional support; perhaps more importantly, he was heading towards Cheshire, which was strongly controlled by the Stanleys, who were pledged to his cause. During the march towards Cardigan the army heard another rumour that Walter Herbert was waiting with a large army at Cardigan ready to oppose Tudor's men. Fortunately for the rebels' peace of mind, this was shown by Henry's scouts to be false. As he marched along, Tudor dispatched messages to people he thought would support him. One such letter, presumably representative of many others, was sent to John ap Maredudd ap Ieun ap Maredudd, an ancestor of the Wynn family of south Carmarthenshire. It is written in a similar style to the letters sent out before the invasion, and was designed to appeal to Welshmen, because as well as declaring that he had come to restore the ancient liberties of England, he promised that he would do the same for Wales. As with the previous letter, it is written as if Tudor were already king:[5]

Right trusty and well beloved, we greet you well. And where it is so that through the help of Almighty God, the assistance of our loving friends and true subjects, and the great confidence that we have to the nobles and commons of this our principality of Wales, we be entered into the same, purposing by the help above rehearsed in all haste possible to descend into our realm of England not only for the adeption of the crown unto us of right appertaining, but also for the oppression of that odious tyrant Richard late Duke of Gloucester, usurper of our said right, and moreover to reduce as well our said realm of England into his ancient estate, honour and prosperity, as this our said principality of Wales, and the people of the same to their original liberties, delivering them of such miserable servitudes as they have piteously long stand in. We desire and pray you and upon your allegiance straitly charge and command you that immediately upon the sight hereof, with all such power as ye may make defensibly arrayed for the war, ye address you towards us without any tarrying upon the way, unto such time as ye be with us wheresoever we shall be to our aid for the effect above rehearsed, wherein ye shall cause us in time to come to be your singular good lord and that ye fail not hereof as ye will avoid our grievous displeasure and answer unto at your peril. Given under our signet …

Henry and his troops probably had not reached Cardigan by 8 August, and tradition says that Henry spent that night at Fagwr Lwyd, about 10 miles from Cardigan. The next day Tudor advanced further into Wales. We do not have certain knowledge of where he was each night, although traditions abound as to the places he stayed at and the magnificent hospitality he enjoyed. It seems likely that these traditions were created well after 1485. We do know that he made very good progress, making forced marches of anything up to 20 miles a day, and advancing via Llwyn Dafydd, Wern Newydd and Aberystwyth. His next certain stopping place was Machynlleth, 92 miles from Cardigan, where he arrived on 14 August. We know this date because it was from here that Tudor wrote a letter to Sir Roger Kynaston, a Shropshire knight. Kynaston was an important landowner in his own right, but more to the purpose at this moment he was in charge of the estates of John Grey, Lord Powis. Grey may have been one of those who had promised Henry aid; according to Henry he certainly was, and it is interesting to note that Grey had been in charge of the troops sent to Brittany by Richard in 1484. Griffiths and Thomas suggest that he may have met Henry then and promised him aid. Tudor needed at least neutrality from Kynaston. This letter still exists and in it Tudor tells Kynaston that Lord Powis had previously offered to help Tudor when he arrived in Wales; he now ordered Kynaston to fulfill this promise 'upon your allegiance', and to assemble Powis's tenants 'defensibly arrayed for the war ye come to us for our aid and assistance in this our enterprise for the recovery of the crown of our realm of England to us of right appertaining'. This message was written 'by the king' and signed 'under our signet beside our town of Machynlleth the 14 day of August'.[6] We do not know how Kynaston responded. He did not receive any subsequent rewards from Tudor, although he remained Sheriff of Merioneth.

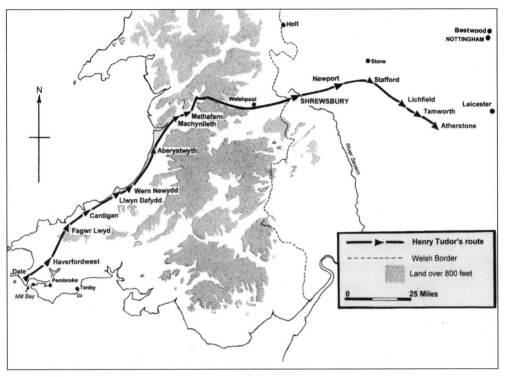

Map 1: Henry Tudor's route to the battlefield. (*Geoffrey Wheeler*)

Small parties of troops had joined Tudor as he progressed through Wales, starting with Richard Griffith, who had deserted Rhys ap Thomas's household, and John Morgan, Tudor's correspondent while in France. At Machynlleth Tudor turned east into central Wales, indicating that he was aiming to cross the Severn at Shrewsbury. At about this time Tudor wrote to, among others, his mother, Lady Margaret Beaufort, and her husband Lord Stanley, to inform them that 'trusting to the aid of his friends' he had determined to pass over the Severn and through Shropshire to go to London and therefore desired them to meet him 'with whom in time and place convenient he would impart more of his intent'. These messages were answered very quickly, we are told, and much money was sent by all of whom it had been asked, being received by

Tudor just as he reached Shrewsbury. His friends all assured him they would be ready to do their duty when the time came. Lord Stanley and his brother had seemingly been gathering troops around them, presumably under the commission given to them by Richard, ready to march into England even if not actually in company with Tudor. Vergil says that Tudor was content with this, although he doubtless thought that more definite promises of support would have been better.[7]

From Machynlleth, Tudor and his army may have passed through Mathafarn, the home of Dafydd Llwyd, one of the most prominent Welsh poets, who praised Tudor after he became king as the foretold saviour of the Welsh nation. By 16 August Tudor and his army were camped at Welshpool. On their way here the rebels at last received sizeable additions to their numbers. Among the newcomers was Rhys Fawr ap Merududd, who brought men and welcome supplies, together with other men from the northern parts of Wales. Finally Rhys ap Thomas came in with his troops, possibly as many as 1,500 of them. Rhys had been shadowing Tudor and his men as they marched across Wales, and the rebel army must have wondered if he was friend or foe. According to Vergil, two days of bargaining had preceded ap Thomas's assurance of loyalty, and Henry promised him the Lieutenancy of Wales in perpetuity. This promise was certainly not fulfilled, but Rhys was knighted three days after Bosworth and received many other posts and rewards, including being elected Knight of the Garter.[8]

On 17 August the rebel army marched to Shrewsbury, where the Welsh gate was firmly shut against them. The Welsh gate was the one by which enemies from Wales were expected to enter the town, and given the nature of Tudor's army, which included Welsh, Scots and Frenchmen, this was not a force to be allowed in without considerable thought and bargaining. Thomas Mitton, the premier burgess, had helped in the arrest of the Duke of Buckingham and Richard had duly rewarded him with the custody of Buckingham's castle at Caus; the king had also reduced the fee farm (money owed to the king) of the town so Mitton must consequently have felt some loyalty to Richard, as is declared by the Shrewsbury Chronicle.[9] Tudor urgently needed to be allowed into the town because if he were to be refused entry here, it would send a message to other English towns that he was not regarded as of great importance and consequently he might encounter more resistance from other towns than might otherwise have been the case. Henry therefore retreated, camped a few miles outside the town and opened further negotiations with the town authorities on the next day, 17 August, assuring them that if his men were allowed to march through the town, he would respect any oaths of loyalty the townspeople had made to Richard III. The negotiations were helped by the arrival of Rowland Warburton, an emissary from Sir William Stanley, who had apparently heard about the impasse at Shrewsbury and decided to take a hand. Stanley's house at Holt in Flintshire was only some 30 miles from Shrewsbury, or he may already have been in the Shrewsbury area with his troops. An agreement was now speedily made with the town, allowing the rebel army to march through, aided by Richard Crompe, or so he claimed afterwards. In November 1485 Crompe, by then one of the marshalls of the royal hall, claimed that he had aided Henry at the risk of his life in his march to Bosworth and 'by his means and diligent labour caused the town of Shrewsbury to be delivered unto your hands'. Crompe certainly received several awards from Henry. Mitton, a man who definitely played an important part in events, does not seem to have suffered politically by his initial resistance to Tudor's entrance, since he was bailiff again in 1488 and several times subsequently.[10]

The rebel army marched on into England, stopping for the night of 18 August at Newport in Shropshire. From here onwards Henry began to be joined by further small bodies of men, two of the most substantial additions being 400 to 500 men under Gilbert Talbot, on behalf of his nephew, the young Earl of Shrewsbury (who may have been with Richard), and 800 men under Sir Richard Corbet, stepson of Sir William Stanley. Talbot's reward was to be knighted on the field after Bosworth and he received much else later. John Mynde of Little Sutton, Shropshire, the son of another John who was probably part of the Talbot entourage, petitioned for a reward in 1487 just after his father died of wounds he had received at the battle. John Mynde the elder had brought six men to the battle, 'defensibly arrayed at his proper cost', but had never received a reward and had died impoverished.[11]

On the next day, 19 August, Tudor marched on to Stafford, where probably that evening he met Sir William Stanley, who apparently reassured Tudor that he would join him with his troops in due time. Sir William had nothing to lose by declaring openly for Tudor, since he had already been declared a traitor (see below), so his refusal to march with Tudor must have seemed suspicious. After their meeting Stanley returned to his troops, who were encamped at Stone, about 8 miles north of Stafford. Tudor then swung south-east, away from the line of march he had adopted hitherto, which would have taken him to Nottingham, and on to a new route which might take him to London. This may have been a feint to deceive Richard into believing that Tudor was going to try to reach London. At Lichfield Tudor again camped outside the town, doubtless to the relief of the citizens, and entered the town on the next day, 20 August. Here he learnt that Lord Stanley had been there some two days earlier, with perhaps as many as 5,000 men. Stanley had moved out of Lichfield as soon as he heard that Tudor was approaching, in order to avoid the appearance of collusion with him and thus arousing the suspicion of the king, and had moved on to Atherstone in Leicestershire. As Tudor must have been well aware, in a long political career Lord Stanley had shown that he was chiefly a supporter of his own interests, and Tudor must have had lingering doubts as to which way Stanley would finally jump. Perhaps Stanley himself was not sure.[12]

In Lichfield Tudor's men were apparently received with great good will and a good time was had by all, even to the firing of guns. Whose guns is not said, although it is unlikely that Tudor would have allowed his men to waste powder at this stage, so if it happened at all, the guns must have been from the town. Indeed, Tudor may have augmented the guns he had brought with him by commandeering the town's weapons when he left.[13] From Lichfield Tudor marched on towards Tamworth, apparently following both Stanleys, who had firstly lagged behind Tudor and were now going ahead of him as if they were fleeing before him. By the time the rebels had arrived in Tamworth on the evening of 20 August, Sir William had moved on to Atherstone, where he conferred with his brother. On the way to Tamworth Tudor was joined by Walter Hungerford and Thomas Bourchier, who had fled from the custody of Sir Robert Brackenbury while he was on his way to join the king. According to Vergil, Tudor was following behind his main army, accompanied by only 20 men, 'sad' and pondering (and doubtless worrying) about the Stanleys' lack of commitment to his cause. He had also heard that the royal army was very well equipped and stood steadfast for the king. While so preoccupied, Tudor apparently lost his way and had to spend the night away from his army, which, it appears, had no idea where he was. Henry is said to have spent the night at a place 3 miles from the main camp of his army. It has been suggested that this was the village of Whittington, 3 miles from Lichfield and half a mile from Tamworth. He found his way back to the army next morning, declaring that he had not been lost but had been conferring with secret friends. If this is true then one of Tudor's escort presumably spoke out of turn, as it seems unlikely that Tudor would have told anyone afterwards. There must have been serious concerns among the senior commanders, who would have concealed the absence of their leader from the main body of the army. If the news had got out that Tudor was missing, then the army might well have disintegrated, as any suspicions or doubts among the soldiers in such a precarious position would not be slow to surface. The whole episode is mysterious and raises the possibility that Tudor had planned to flee, despairing of his chances, but had been persuaded to change his mind.[14]

Tudor now went to Atherstone to talk with the Stanley brothers. Tradition has it that they met in the Three Tuns public house, but it is rather more likely that they met at Merevale Abbey nearby. It seems the meeting was a cheerful one, with the participants 'taking one another by the hand and yielding mutual salutation each man was glad for the good state of the others and all their minds were moved to great joy. After that they entered in counsel in what sort to do battle with King Richard', although Vergil does not say what the conclusion was and it is apparent that Tudor still did not know what the Stanley brothers had in mind. It must have been obvious to him that if anything went wrong for his forces during the battle, they would probably take sides with the king. After this episode Tudor returned to his camp at Tamworth, where a group of knights, John Savage, Brian Sandford and Simon Digby, came to him with some more men for his army. All of them were men whom Richard had recruited to his own forces, so their arrival in Tudor's camp was very welcome. All received rewards during the reign of Henry VII but only Savage received a grant 'in consideration of his having largely exposed himself, with a crowd of his kinsmen, servants and friends, as volunteers in the king's service, in the battle against the king's great adversary Richard III, the late pretended King of England'.[15]

At some point, either before or after the conference with the Stanleys, Tudor marched his army to Atherstone, camping for the night of 20 August a little way from Thomas Stanley, who may have been as little as a mile or so to the north of the rebel army. Sir William was perhaps the same distance to the south. Legend again says that Tudor lodged at the Three Tuns public house in Atherstone, but it is more likely that he lodged in the Cistercian abbey of Merevale, which is about a mile west of Atherstone, with his men around or nearby. Certainly he recompensed the abbey very soon after the battle. On 7 December 1485, 'because he [the Abbot] had sustained great hurts charges and losses by occasion of the great repair and resort that our people coming toward our late field as well unto the house of Merevale aforesaid as in going over his ground to the destruction of his corns and pastures', compensation totalling 100 marks was paid to the abbey 'in ready money', and the abbot afterwards received a reward of 10 marks. It is apparent that several thousand troops did a lot of damage in the two days they were there. Atherstone itself received a grant of £24 13s 4d in recompense for losses of corn and grain 'by us and our company at our late victorious field for destruction'. A grant (also in ready money) was also made to other villages in the area (see below).[16]

The next day, Sunday, 21 August, according to the Ballad of Bosworth Field, the two Stanleys made their battle plans, and agreed to amalgamate their forces. Lord Stanley would command the vanguard and Sir William Stanley the rearguard, with Sir Edward Stanley, Sir William's son, commanding one wing.[17] This seems most unlikely, since Sir William had already been declared a traitor, and for Lord Stanley to join with his brother at this stage would effectively have meant he was declaring himself to be a traitor too. Whatever the arrangements, it appears that on Sunday, 21 August the rebel armies of both Tudor and the Stanleys stayed in their various camps around Atherstone. It has been said by many authors, following Hutton, that on 21 August Tudor and the Stanleys marched towards Richard's camp and camped at Whitemoors, about a mile east of the village of Upton.[18] However, no archaeological traces of a camp have been found at Whitemoors and it therefore seems more likely that the rebel armies remained in their camps at or near Atherstone on the Sunday. For Tudor's men at least a rest must have been most welcome after their rapid march. Many of them had landed on 7 August and had been more or less continuously on the move since then.

Chapter 4

Preparing to Receive the Invader

As soon as he received the news of Tudor's invasion, Richard reacted swiftly and galvanised everyone in the royal household into frantic activity. He already had with him some troops and leading supporters, such as his heir the Earl of Lincoln, but now letters began flooding out from Nottingham to his other supporters. The first that we know of was sent to Henry Vernon, squire of the body, telling him about Tudor's landing in Wales: 'our rebels and traitors accompanied with our ancient enemies France and other strange nations departed out of the water of Seine the first day of this present month making their course westwards been landed at Nangle besides Milford Haven in Wales on Sunday last past', that is, 7 August. (As discussed above, Tudor is more likely to have landed at Dale, on the opposite side of the harbour.) The letter to Vernon commanded him to join the king in person as soon as possible, together with the number of men he had promised previously 'sufficiently horsed and harnessed'. As well as writing to supporters such as Vernon, Richard also wrote to major supporters such as the Duke of Norfolk, who promptly wrote to their own retainers. Norfolk wrote to John Paston, one of his tenants, on Friday, 12 (or Saturday, 13) August, commanding him to join him at Bury St Edmunds where Norfolk would be on Tuesday, 16 August, with the men he had promised the king together with as many others as he could gather, 'and I pray you ordain them jackets of my livery'. Norfolk had been informed that the king intended to set out from Nottingham on the Tuesday after Lady Day, that is, 16 August. The city of York knew about the invasion by 16 August, and possibly earlier, and on that day the council agreed to send John Spooner, sergeant of the mace, and John Nicholson (one of the officers of the mace) to the king in

Nottingham to ask how many troops he wanted them to send to him. They further proclaimed that all freemen of the city should be ready in 'their most defensible array' at an hour's notice. It is strange that York does not seem to have received an official letter commanding the city to gather its troops. Presumably they should have heard through the commissioners of array, who would have received instructions from the king, but it seems the message did not get through. Kendall has suggested that the Earl of Northumberland, who perhaps later betrayed Richard, deliberately failed to inform the authorities in York on the grounds that he did not want troops loyal to the king in his northern levies. This is possible, if a little unlikely. In the event, although Northumberland did bring a sizeable body of men to the battle, they did not strike a blow for Richard or indeed for anyone else. It seems most likely that inefficiency was the reason why York was not told officially, but the authorities there obviously found out by some means.[1] It seems very unlikely that either Vernon or John Paston obeyed the appeals. Vernon had received no fewer than six appeals from the Duke of Clarence and the Earl of Warwick to bring men to support them in 1471 and refused them all, and Paston was appointed Sheriff of Norfolk and Suffolk not long after Bosworth, which probably indicates that he had not appeared for the king at the battle.[2] Richard also summoned Sir Robert Brackenbury, Lieutenant of the Tower, probably ordering him to bring the tower ordnance with him. Vergil says that he was told to bring with him Thomas Bourchier, Walter Hungerford and others whom Richard did not trust. As we have already noted, Bourchier and Hungerford deserted Brackenbury just after they reached Stony Stratford and did indeed later join Tudor's army.[3]

Certainly the news of Tudor's landing was distributed very efficiently: it had been received within a very few days by Vernon in Derbyshire, by the Duke of Norfolk in East Anglia and in York in the north. It has been claimed that the news travelled about 400 miles from west Wales to East Anglia in just seven days, an astonishing achievement. News was travelling to and from the north very fast too: York heard back from the king in a report by John Nicolson on 19 August, just three days after they sent Spooner and Nicolson to him. The council discussed the report and agreed to send 80 men to Richard, ordering that they 'should in all haste depart towards the king's grace for the subduing of his enemies aforesaid'. They appointed the afternoon of the same day to choose the men and give them their wages of 10 shillings each for ten days' service. These wages were paid by the parish from which each man came. Despite their haste, the men of York would not arrive in time, although given the distances and the time needed to reach the various rendezvous, the troops must all have been mounted. The rate of payment to the York troops seems to bear that out, and although they still did not get there in time, they cannot have been very far away. A journey of about two days on horseback, even on poor roads, must have brought them very close to the battlefield. Spooner had apparently stayed with the king; we do not know if he fought in the battle but if so, he certainly survived because he reported the result to the York council on the day after, 23 August. The council recorded in their minutes how they had received the official news of Richard's death, and immediately afterwards commented that since the troops had only been away for four and a half days, not the ten for which they had been paid, they should be allowed wages for six days but no more and the rest of the money should be repaid to the parishes from which it had come.[4]

In Nottingham all must have been disciplined activity as the king marshalled the troops as they arrived and organised his commanders. Lord Stanley, whose troops should have been mustering in Cheshire and Lancashire ready to resist the advance of Tudor, is said to have asked permission, probably in early July, before the actual invasion took place, to go to Lancashire, 'his native home and family from who he had been long away'. The Crowland Chronicler says that the king refused to allow him to make a long stay there unless he sent his son Lord Strange to the king in his place, as a kind of hostage for good behaviour. Richard suspected, with good cause, that Stanley was plotting to support Tudor when the time came, and Stanley may have known that Tudor intended to sail as soon as he could. We know that Lord Strange was in Nottingham on 1 August, as he witnessed the arrival of the Great Seal on that day, and since Lord Stanley did not, he was presumably not in Nottingham. When the news of the rebels' landing arrived, Richard is said to have demanded

Stanley's return to Nottingham. The devious Stanley refused on the grounds that he had the sweating sickness, which may have been true as it was undoubtedly present in England. Lord Strange then apparently tried to leave Nottingham clandestinely but 'was discovered by a snare and seized'. He then 'revealed a conspiracy to support the party of the Earl of Richmond between himself, his uncle William Stanley and Sir John Savage [Lord Stanley's nephew], asked for mercy and promised that his father would come to the king's aid as fast as possible, with all his power'. In addition he wrote to his father describing the danger he was in, and expressing the urgent need to bring help to the king.[5] Lord Strange's predicament was undoubtedly the reason why Stanley and his brother Sir William did not openly join the rebels until the end of the battle. Richard had already made up his mind about Sir William by this point, however, and declared him a traitor, together with Sir John Savage, the sentence being declared in Coventry and (presumably) other towns.[6]

However, there is reason to doubt at least part of this traditional story. A quitclaim from Bewsey, Warrington, dated 18 July 1485, was witnessed by, among others, both Lord Stanley and Strange, showing that they were both in Lancashire in the middle of July – in other words Stanley was probably not at court at that time.[7] Stanley at least should have been in Lancashire, carrying out Richard's orders to gather troops, and Strange did later go to Nottingham to be with the king, presumably in accordance with the king's order. But the Crowland Chronicler says that when Stanley asked to leave court, the king insisted that Lord Strange came to court before allowing Stanley to leave, which is certainly not what happened. That Richard must have mistrusted the Stanley family is undeniable. Whatever the situation, they always seemed to come out on the winning side. In addition, Stanley was married to Margaret Beaufort, who had been thoroughly implicated in the Buckingham uprising. However, Richard had little choice but to hope that they would be loyal to him when it came to battle, and overtly holding Strange as a hostage was obviously a risky strategy that might provoke even greater animosity. Stanley can have been in no doubt about the risk he was taking with the life of his son. He knew that Yorkist kings could be quite ruthless when it suited them, as illustrated by the death of Lord Welles in 1470. Edward IV had pardoned Welles earlier in the year but when he heard that Welles's son Sir Robert was in arms against him, Edward ordered Welles to tell his son to lay down his arms or Welles's own life would be forfeit. Sir Robert did not disperse his army but confronted the king's army with his own. Edward then executed Lord Welles in front of both armies.[8]

However, whatever the Stanleys were going to do, by the weekend of 14/15 August Richard knew he had to start his march towards his oncoming enemy. He must have realised that his army was not yet complete (we have seen how the York men only left their city on 19 or 20 August), but he could not wait any longer. He therefore marched out of Nottingham towards Leicester very early on Friday, 19 August, later than forecast by the Duke of Norfolk in his letter to Paston. The army was in 'square battle' formation, as Vergil calls it, with the king and his household following the baggage train, all between wings of cavalry, and presumably with a vanguard preceding them. They arrived in Leicester 'a little before sunset' that day. Here the royal forces were probably joined by Norfolk and his son the Earl of Surrey with their East Anglian levies, by Sir Robert Brackenbury, Constable of the Tower, with his troops from London, and lastly by the Earl of Northumberland with his troops. Brackenbury almost certainly brought guns from the Tower armoury. Richard stayed in Leicester for two days, traditionally staying in the White Boar inn in Northgate Street but more likely staying at the castle, which was then habitable and from where he had sent a letter on 18 August 1483. After the battle the White Boar became the Blue Boar inn, after the badge of the Earl of Oxford, one of Tudor's commanders.[9] Vergil says that Richard left Nottingham on the same day that Tudor arrived at Lichfield, which seems correct. Richard knew of Tudor's movements through his scouts, or 'scurriers'.[10]

On Sunday, 21 August, with his army as complete as he could make it, Richard marched out of Leicester to meet the advancing rebel army. The York levy had still not reached him, and there must have been others also still marching towards a battle that would be over before they arrived. The king had not been joined by either Lord Stanley or his brother Sir

William, which must have worried him. They, of course, had been marching in front of Tudor's army, ostensibly to cover his advance, but Richard must have known of the contact between the Stanleys and Tudor, and must surely have wondered when they would show their hand and how.

The royal army would have been a magnificent sight as it marched out of Leicester, probably with the chief officers in full armour and with heraldic banners displayed. Richard himself wore a coronet on his helmet. His heralds rode before him, and he was surrounded by his chief officers, Norfolk, Surrey and Northumberland, and by his Household officers, perhaps Lord Lovell his Chamberlain, Sir Robert Percy, William Catesby and his secretary John Kendall. There is a legend that as he rode past Richard's heel scraped along the parapet of Bow Bridge over the river Soar and a wise woman sitting there prophesied that when he returned his head would strike the same spot.

Richard knew that Tudor was at Atherstone and so directed his march in that direction, heading west out of Leicester and probably following the old Roman road, the Fosse Way, towards Watling Street. He needed a good road to allow faster movement and to make moving the baggage train and above all the guns easier, and it seems likely that the old Roman road was still better than any other available. With Tudor at Atherstone, which was on Watling Street, the road to London, Richard needed to be in a position to intercept any possible advance towards the capital. The Fosse Way, now known as Fenn Lane, intercepted Watling Street nearly 2 miles from Atherstone. Richard probably took this route to see where the rebels would go next. If Tudor continued towards London, then Richard was in a position to swing down and cut him off, but if Tudor headed for Leicester, then Richard only had to choose a good battleground and wait for him. Richard's scouts would have reported to him during the course of the day that Tudor was still at Atherstone, and thus still on the road towards Leicester. The royal army thus continued in a westerly direction. If the Roman road was still usable this far from Leicester, it would have taken the royal forces through Kirkby Mallory, and they probably camped near the village of Sutton Cheney, perhaps on

Ambion Hill itself, which lies at the end of the ridge on which Sutton Cheney sits. If the Fosse Way was not usable, then there were other roads to get to the same destination.[11]

Sutton Cheney lies on a ridge of high ground about 12 miles from Leicester. It seems a likely site, as from here Richard would have been in sight of the road to London and very near to the Fosse Way to Leicester, so he could have intercepted Tudor whichever way he went. However, there is no contemporary evidence that he camped here. The later chronicler Raphael Holinshed, writing in 1577, said that he camped on 'Anne Beame' hill, but this name is not in his sources and it is not known where it comes from. The only evidence that troops were quartered in or near Sutton Cheney is the large number of finds of possibly related materials found there as part of the Bosworth survey.[12] One contemporary source, the Crowland Chronicle, says that Richard camped on the night of 21 August about 8 miles from Leicester, near Merevale Abbey. Ambion Hill is actually about 9 statute miles from Leicester. The old English mile was about 1.3 statute miles, so in effect the Crowland Chronicler is saying that Richard camped about 7 miles from Leicester. It seems probable that the Crowland Chronicler was not present at the battle, as his account of the events on 22 August is very sketchy. He seems to have been an eye-witness to the events he described up to this point, so perhaps he and other clerics were left behind in Leicester, and therefore was reporting on something without having witnessed it for himself. His estimate of distance is therefore a reasonable one.[13] Wherever they stopped for the night, Richard's men pitched their tents and found refreshments, and Richard 'with many words exhorted them to the fight to come', as Polydore Vergil says. Richard had certainly arranged for their refreshment, since we know that supplies consisting of bread and ale to the value of £6 8s 9d were sent to the camp from Coventry. Perhaps the Thomas Maideford noted in the Coventry accounts as having later received 2s 6d for the hurt he suffered 'in the field' had carried the provisions to the field and somewhat injudiciously stayed to see (or even take part in) the battle. Probably other places sent food too.[14] It remains possible that Richard camped for the night of 21 August on the site where he intended to fight the following day, on the plain below Ambion Hill. It is probable that some of Richard's troops were quartered away from the hill, as several thousand men occupied a lot of space. The guns would certainly not have been hauled up the hill, and must have been parked under strong guard near the bottom.

Chapter 5

Military Matters

The Size of the Rebel and Royal Armies

The rival armies were very different in size. To some extent we are more sure about the size of the rebel army than we are of the king's. As seen above, when Henry Tudor left Wales we know that he had with him his English exiles, perhaps some 400 of them, although the figure is sometimes said to be as high as 500 to 600. Then there were his French troops. Molinet says that the King of France had supplied Tudor with 1,800 men and that Tudor then recruited another 1,800 at Harfleur just before he set sail. It seems unlikely that the two figures would have been exactly the same, so perhaps Molinet is mistaken and Tudor recruited fewer on his own account. He could not have afforded to pay too many men, but perhaps there were between 2,000 and 3,600 French troops. Tudor also had some Scotsmen from the King of France's army, although we do not know how many. The later Scots chroniclers say they made up 1,000 men from the total of 6,000 men given to Tudor by Charles, but this number seems absurdly high. About 300, plus the French troops, may be more likely.

In conclusion, Tudor landed in Wales with perhaps 4,000 men in all; this is twice the number of 2,000 that Vergil attributes to him, although Vergil may have deliberately understated the number to emphasise how brilliantly Tudor triumphed with so few men. This number of men would fit reasonably well, if not comfortably, into the twenty ships that Tudor was apparently given by Charles.[1] So Tudor probably had at least 5,000 men with him by the time he reached Bosworth, the roughly 4,000 he landed with having been bolstered by the men brought to him by Rhys ap Thomas and the 500 brought by Gilbert Talbot, plus those small parties of Welsh and Englishmen who joined him during the march.

The Castilian Report says that Tudor had 5,000 men when he landed in Wales, 2,000 from Charles VIII (paid up for four months) and 3,000 English exiles. This total of 5,000 men is probably the number estimated to be on the battlefield by Juan de Salazar, who was with Richard. Salazar was a prominent and successful captain who had been in England before and was probably there now to aid Richard with the permission of Maximilian, King of the Romans, who was anxious about the expansion of French influence.[2]

It is much more difficult to estimate numbers for the royal army. Richard's men were not raised by indenture, as would have been the case with a foreign war (which would give us specific numbers), and we do not know how many men responded to the letters he sent out. We know that the Duke of Norfolk responded, although we do not know if those men he in turn wrote to also obeyed the summons. Nor do we know how many men the various commissioners of array raised. As noted above, the commissioners had been ordered to put their men on an hour's notice, so that it should have been possible to raise a goodly number from the areas around Nottingham and Leicester at least, and given the speed of the spread of news it should have been possible for troops, particularly if mounted, to come from further afield. The men of York only left on 20 August, but since they were mounted they would not have been very far from Bosworth when the battle took place, and bodies of troops from nearer at hand would surely have been able to join the royal army in time.

Preserved in various records is a small amount of circumstantial evidence suggesting that a skirmish took place near Bosworth on or about 20 August, two days before the actual battle. Boatwright and Baldwin have pointed out that six tenants-in-chief (that is, men holding lands directly from the king and thus men of some status) are recorded in the Inquisitions Post Mortem for the first year of Henry VII as having died on 20 August 1485.[3] Such inquisitions were always held when tenants-in-chief died, in order to make inquiries into what the king might be entitled to claim from their estates. The actual date of death was determined by the inquisitions as accurately as possible. The deaths of the six tenants-in-chief on 20 August may be compared with the 16 such deaths that occurred on 22 and 23 August, presumably as a direct result of the battle. It is possible, of course, that the families of the men recorded as having died on 20 August were trying to avoid the risk of their estates being attainted (the dead men having technically committed treason against their new lawful sovereign), although this seems unlikely to be the case for all of them. However, one of the men recorded as dying on 20 August was Richard Boughton, Sheriff of Warwickshire and Leicestershire. It seems possible that Boughton was killed on 20 August when the forces he had raised in response to the commission of array were involved in a skirmish with the gathering rebel forces. Of the other five men recorded as dying before the battle, four are from Essex and Suffolk, and could have been retainers of the Earl of Oxford, one of Tudor's main commanders, but one, John Kebell, a commissioner of array, of Rearsby in Leicestershire, is recorded as dying on 21 August. His date of death could be a ploy to avoid a charge of treason, but he could perhaps have been seriously wounded in the skirmish.

If Boughton had duly raised his troops, then it seems very likely that other commissioners would also have done so, particularly in the counties around Nottingham, from where the king's final instructions came. Thus men would have been raised from the Midland counties of Nottinghamshire, Warwickshire, Leicestershire and probably Northamptonshire, as well as from the nearer parts of more distant counties such as Oxfordshire, Gloucestershire, Buckinghamshire and south Yorkshire. Mounted men would quite easily have been able to get to the muster point in time. We do not know how many men would be raised from each shire, but we do know that Bridport in Dorset, at that time with a population of about 500 all told, mustered 201 men between the ages of 16 and 60 (the legal ages to be liable for service), fit and able to bear arms, in response to a commission of array of 1457. If this number could be raised by one small town, it seems likely that at least 1,000 could be raised from a shire.[4] We also know that in February 1484 the Duke of Norfolk undertook to raise from his estates nearly 760 men, all at his own wages, and presumably he would have done the same in

1485.[5] In addition, he would certainly have seen to it that the commissioners of array in Essex, Suffolk and Norfolk did their duty. We thus have at least, say, 1,500 men (and quite possibly more) from this one source. If all of the counties listed above could raise half of this figure each, then the king would have had perhaps 8,000 men plus those brought by other retainers, and plus those amassed by the Earl of Northumberland, who was bringing the levies of Yorkshire, Cumberland and Westmorland, or as many as he could raise in the time. This would have given a total of perhaps 10,000 men, but this might be an optimistic estimate so it would be safer to say about 8,000 men. It has been said that Richard would have been better prepared in 1484 than he was in 1485. In terms of being theoretically ready for an invasion he may well have been, but the critical factor was the ability to get soldiers to the battlefield and we have no reason to suppose that more men could have responded more quickly in 1484 than in 1485.

The Stanley Forces

Lord Stanley has been often credited with having as many as 5,000 men, but given that Richard had ordered the men of Lancashire and Cheshire to put themselves at the disposal of the two Stanley brothers, this seems a very modest number for him to have raised. He would probably have heard of Tudor's landing very soon after it had happened. One of the Stanleys certainly raised troops from the city of Chester, as the sheriffs here were afterwards allowed a reduction of their fee farm since they had sent troops to help Henry in his 'victorious journey'. Depending on which side he chose to support, Stanley obviously had the capacity either to even up the fight or to make one army overwhelmingly larger than the other. Vergil says that Sir William had 3,000 men under his command.[6] Obviously Vergil might have downplayed the numbers of rebel troops and overplayed the numbers of the royal army, but given the speed at which the men had to be raised, and the fact that it was harvest time, when men would be reluctant to serve in any army, these figures seem reasonable.

Equipment and Weapons

The medieval army contained a mixture of specialists and generalists. They were not armed with a uniform set of equipment, or indeed uniforms, although such things were becoming known on the continent; Charles the Bold, Duke of Burgundy, for example, ordered that his troops should wear surcoats of blue and white, his livery colours, with the Burgundian red cross of St Andrew on the breast.[7] This type of universal provision was not known at that time in England but the men in a given lord's retinue may well have worn his livery, as did those of the Duke of Norfolk. The men of Sir William Stanley are said by the Ballad of the Lady Bessy to have worn red jackets, while those of Sir John Savage wore white hoods, according both to the Ballad of Lady Bessy and the Ballad of Bosworth Field.[8] Even so, to modern eyes, a medieval army would have looked like a scruffy and disorganised rabble. There were sometimes foreign mercenaries in a medieval army. We have no evidence that Richard's army included any, although perhaps some of his handgunners were mercenaries and someone lost the Burgundian double patards found recently, see plates. We do know, however, that there were many mercenaries in Tudor's army.

English armies of this period always included three arms, of which the infantry was the most numerous. These included archers and 'spearmen', i.e., men armed with staff weapons. These spearmen carried a variety of staff weapons, as well as spears, in England frequently bills (the familiar bill-hook with a long hooked blade, of the type still used for lopping hedges, etc.), glaives (with a long knife-like blade attached to a staff), and poleaxes, which had an axe blade on one side and one of a variety of deadly back spikes. The wielders of these weapons were the least skilled of the troops, although that is not to say they were unskilled. Their weapons were all dangerous in the hands of a skilled man. The great majority of the infantry usually comprised the archers, equipped with the English (and Welsh) longbow. In English armies it was common to have a high proportion of archers, which heavily outnumbered the other infantry. Edward IV took eight archers for every man-at-arms on his French expedition in 1475, but that was in an army that had been long in preparation and was raised by indenture, so that the numbers that each commander would bring was organised beforehand. A ratio of three to one would be more usual.[9] Vergil says that the archers were put in the front of the vanguard, and that Richard put Norfolk in charge of the archers, and presumably in command of the whole vanguard. If they covered the whole length of the van, which Vergil says was of a 'wonderful length', the implication is that there must have been a goodly number of them. Out of a total of 201 men-at-arms in Bridport in 1457, there were 114 who brought a long bow to the muster. The English archer was rightly feared as a warrior. Mancini says that the English bows and arrows were 'thicker and longer than those used by other nations, just as their bodies are stronger than other peoples' for they seem to have hands and arms of iron'.[10] Both archers and spearmen carried a short sword or long dagger as well as their main weapon. Archers were also skilled at using these weapons, and could be used as lightly armed infantry when necessary, for example in hand-to-hand fighting in the final stages of a battle.

The foot soldiers always wore some form of protection, which might be almost as much as full armour, but most of them wore a helmet (probably a sallet type, which resembled a modern steel helmet but often had a visor), perhaps mail sleeves and a brigandine. This was a thick, padded jacket, which consisted of small plates of metal riveted to the inside of a fabric covering (of leather or strong canvas), and covered on the outside with fabric, perhaps velvet or silk if the owner was wealthy. The jack was a rather similar garment, and consisted of small plates of metal or horn secured between layers of canvas by a trellis-work of stitches. Some common soldiers merely wore a doublet of some kind, padded with straw or rags, and some had simple mail shirts. Mostly soldiers were expected to provide military equipment at their own expense, although some lords equipped the men they raised from their estates and some towns had a stock of communal weapons and armour that could be given to the levies that they were called on to provide. In these cases the costs were sometimes taken out of the soldiers' wages.

Another unknown factor is how many of each type of non-knightly mounted troops were represented in the royal army. Probably most of the

Richard III, portrait painted soon after 1510. This is probably the earliest surviving copy of a portrait painted in Richard's lifetime. (*Reproduced by permission of the Society of Antiquaries of London*)

Portrait of John Howard (d. 1485), Duke of Norfolk, from a painting on glass formerly at Tendring Hall, Suffolk. (*Geoffrey Wheeler*)

(*Opposite*) Drawing of the lost brass of Thomas Howard (d. 1524), Earl of Surrey, formerly in Lambeth Church. (*Geoffrey Wheeler*)

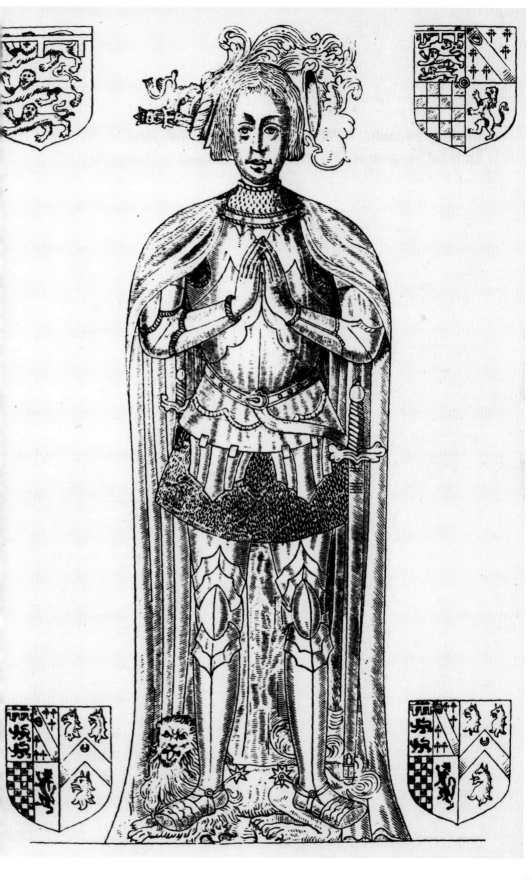

Garter stall plate of Henry Stafford, Duke of Buckingham. (*Geoffrey Wheeler*)

Garter stall plate of Francis, Viscount Lovell. (*Geoffrey Wheeler*)

Effigy of Rhys ap Thomas (d. 1525), in St Peter's Church, Carmarthen.
(*Geoffrey Wheeler*)

Drawing of the seal of Jasper Tudor, Earl of Pembroke and Duke of Bedford.
(*Geoffrey Wheeler*)

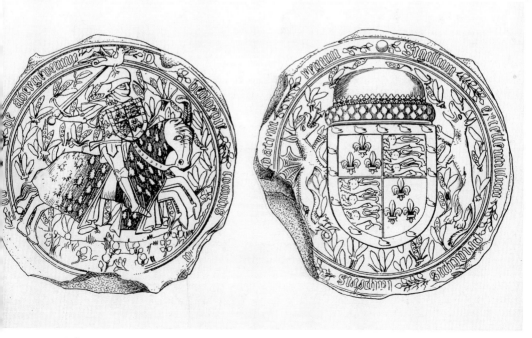

The cairn over King Dicks Well, Ambion Hill, photographed in the 1930s before restoration.

(*Opposite, top*) Crown Hill from Ambion Hill in the 1930s. Stoke Golding Church is in the background.

(*Opposite, bottom*) Crown Hill with Stoke Golding Church in the background. (*Geoffrey Wheeler*)

Effigy of Sir John Cheyne
(d. 1509) in Salisbury Cathedral
(*Geoffrey Wheeler*)

Garter stall plate of Henry
Percy, Earl of Northumberland
(*Geoffrey Wheeler*)

Mourner representing Sir John Savage (d. 1492), with one of his sisters, on the tomb of his father in Macclesfield Church, Cheshire. (*Geoffrey Wheeler*)

The Bosworth cross, from the drawing by Thomas Sharp, 1793. (*Geoffrey Wheeler*)

Effigies in Ormskirk Church, thought to represent Lord Stanley and (perhaps) his first wife Eleanor Neville. (*Geoffrey Wheeler*)

(*Opposite*) Henry VII, portrait of about 1501.
(*Reproduced by permission of the Society of Antiquaries of London*)

The new site of the battle of Bosworth, looking north west towards the hedge bordering Fenn Lane and across the marsh. (*Lynda Pidgeon*)

Central panel from a late sixteenth-century carving of the battle of Bosworth, showing Henry VII trampling the fallen figure of Richard III holding the crown. Supporters of Richard, including the Duke of Norfolk, are on the right, and those of Henry, including the Earl of Oxford, are on the left. (*Geoffrey Wheeler*)

A small (28mm long) silver gilt boar badge found on the new site of the battle.
(*Leicestershire County Council*)

Coins found near the new site of the battle: (*right*) a double patard of Burgundy and
(*left*) a groat of Edward IV. (*Leicestershire County Council*)

The grave of Richard III in Greyfriars Priory, Leicester. (*University of Leicester*)

(*Opposite*) Shot and hand gun pellets found on the new site of the battle. (*Leicestershire County Council*)

Reconstruction of the head of Richard III from the excavated skull. (*Richard III Society*)

levies coming from a distance would be mounted, as the York levies certainly were. Mancini says that English troops were not 'accustomed to fight from horseback but because they use horses to carry them to the scene of the engagement, so as to arrive fresher and not tired by the fatigue of the journey therefore they will ride any sort of horse, even pack horses'. This may not have been as universally true as Mancini implies, although some of the battles and skirmishes that took place during the Wars of the Roses were fast moving and some were decided by cavalry action, as was the case at Tewkesbury in 1471 and indeed Bosworth.[11] There were certainly some lightly armed horsemen in the armies, since the commissions of array specifically mentioned them as a category, and these presumably remained mounted during the battle. They could be used to guard the wings of the army, as they did on Richard's march from Nottingham, or deployed as a shock force during the battle, as they were at the battle of Tewkesbury. They were also used as scurriers, or scouts, sent forward to detect the presence of enemy forces or perhaps observe their advance. They sometimes acted as forward troops to secure an advanced position, as Edward IV's men did just before the battle of Barnet, when they drove the Earl of Warwick's forces out of the village of Barnet.

At the very top of the medieval army were the commanders, all mounted men from the knightly class. Not all were necessarily knights as such, but as a group they were drawn from the gentry and the peerage, and even wealthier merchants. How many of these there were in the army is debatable but probably they numbered in the very low hundreds. The better equipped of these commanders were fully protected in plate armour and they carried an array of weapons. Most of these well-armed men followed the English practice of fighting on foot, but as we shall see Richard apparently retained a group of armed mounted men for use as a reserve. The cavalry charge was still sometimes used at the end of a battle to deliver the final crushing blow to a defeated enemy, and Richard attempted to use it for this purpose at Bosworth.

Putting on plate armour was an elaborate process and required time. There is a surviving fifteenth-century description of the full process entitled 'How a man shall be armed at his ease when he shall fight on foot':[12]

> He shall have no shirt upon him but a doublet of fustian lined with satin cut full of holes. The doublet must be strongly sewn where the points must be set about the upper part of the arm and breast before and behind, and gussets of mail must be sewn to the doublet at the bend of the arm and under the arm. The arming points must be made of fine twine such as men use to make strings for crossbows, and they must be tied small and pointed as points. Also they must be waxed with shoemakers' wax, and they will neither stretch nor break. He shall have a pair of hose of worsted cloth, and a pair of short pads of thin blanket to put about his knees against the chafing of his leg harness; also a pair of shoes of thick leather, and they must be fastened with small whip-cord, three knots upon a cord, and three cords must be sewn fast unto the heel of the shoe and fine cords in the middle of the sole of the same shoe, and there must be between the cords of the heel and those of the middle of the shoe the space of three fingers.

The description then goes on to 'arming a man'. It is interesting to see here how much thought had been given to easing the drawing of weapons. The sword given to the man at the end would very probably have been replaced by a long hafted poleaxe in English battles. When fighting on foot, the sword, if worn, would probably be left in its scabbard (or ring):

> First you must put on sabatons [foot armour] and tie them upon the shoe with small points that will not break. And then greaves [leg armour] and cuisses [thigh armour] and the breach of mail [to protect the loins], and the tonlets [laminated skirts to protect the abdomen] and the breast-plate, and the vambraces [to protect the forearms] and the rerebraces [to protect the upper arms], and then the gloves. Then hang his dagger upon his right side, and his short sword on his left side in a round ring quite naked so that he can pull it out easily. Then put his surcoat on his back. Then put his bascinet [helmet] on his shoulders

and fasten it to the breast by two staples in front and with a double buckle on the back to make the bascinet keep in exactly the right position. And then his long sword in his hand and then his pennant in his hand painted of St George or of Our Lady to bless him as he goes towards the field and in the field.

Guns

Armies of the late fifteenth century increasingly included artillerymen, handgunners or men trained to handle larger guns, as by this time artillery was regarded as an important part of a military force. Edward IV took an impressive artillery train to France in 1475 and we have seen that Richard took steps to organise his own artillery train at the Tower of London. The act of attainder against Richard and his leading men described the royal army as equipped with 'guns, bows, arrows, spears, glaives, axes and all other weaponry'. The guns would have been brought by Brackenbury from the Tower and must have been those that Richard had so carefully organised. These guns were the lighter and slightly more manageable field artillery on their own light wheeled carriages, not the large, impressive and difficult to manoeuvre siege guns. The Ballad of Bosworth Field says that Richard had chained 140 serpentines in a line, presumably both to concentrate their fire and to create a barrier – an interesting idea but unlikely. Serpentines were small guns, probably firing a ball of about 2 inches in diameter. Proof that guns like this were used was found on the battlefield in the form of 22 roundshot from guns of this calibre. One of the balls found was of sufficient size (just over 3 inches in width, or 93 mm) to show that it came from one of the large guns called sakers, which could be anything up to 9 feet long (2.75 m) and correspondingly heavy.[13] The Ballad of Bosworth Field says that the king also had larger guns known as bombards, although there is no physical evidence for their presence at Bosworth, and harquebusiers with their handguns, that is hackbuts.[14] It is possible that these harquebusiers had come with the Spanish knight Salazar, who was present on the field with the king, but we know that Richard had purchased 28 hackbuts. These small guns fired large lead pellets and were sometimes supported on a kind of tripod. Their gunpowder had to be of a better quality than that used for larger guns. There is no doubt that Henry Tudor had hand gunners at the battle since two small lead pellets, which can only have come from a small calibre weapon such as a hand gun, have been found on the position occupied by the royal army – that is, had been fired at them. Tudor presumably used guns provided by the French king. Molinet also says that Richard had guns, implying they were probably small calibre.[15] Although the guns were clumsy and rather difficult to manoeuvre once they had been positioned on the battlefield, particularly if they were on soft ground into which the wheels would sink, they were highly valued, perhaps because of their ability to shock and awe the opposing troops, most of whom would not have seen or heard them before. How much effect the guns had on the result of the battle we may never know, and the final outcome was determined by an old-fashioned cavalry charge, but the guns may have played a part in bringing about the situation where the charge became necessary.

Handgunners, as depicted in a medieval manuscript. (*Geoffrey Wheeler*)

Troop Organisation and Deployment

Having got a body of troops to the battlefield, their deployment by the commanders needs a little thought. Any army needs a structure to function in combat; the men cannot just mill about in a formless mass. It seems probable that the army structures used at Bosworth owed at least something to continental practice, developed first in France and then in Burgundy. Given the close links between England and Burgundy at this time (Margaret, Duchess of Burgundy was the sister of Edward IV and Richard III), it seems most likely that a version of Burgundian practice was employed. In essence, although numbers could vary widely, the army was divided into companies of about 100 archers and 100 men–at–arms, and each company had a captain and a standard.[16] This arrangement also enabled men to be kept in order during a march. The commissions of array say that the men raised under the commissions should be arranged in thousands, hundreds and scores, and presumably the divisions (usually called 'battles' at this time) into which the armies were divided were broken down into smaller groups at Bosworth. In many cases, in England at least, the smaller units would probably have been under their own lords, with their own banners. We know that the Earl of Oxford, commanding the rebel army, ordered his men at one stage in the battle not to go more than 10 feet from the standards, and later arranged the men into an attacking triangle (see below), which implies small units of about a hundred men. This attacking formation is one that was used on the continent, where Oxford may have heard of it.

The amount of space that a given body of men would occupy also needed to be known by a commander. Unless some estimate can be made of the amount of ground that a given number of troops take up, it is not possible to sensibly decide whether the force could occupy it or not. Vegetius's late Roman textbook on warfare, armies and strategy,[17] which was widely used in the Middle Ages and later, and books derived from it, say that each man on foot occupies a space 3 feet wide and 7 feet deep (or less when in close order). Contamine quotes a Swiss source as showing that a Swiss square of 10,000 men in the regular formation of the late fifteenth century occupied a space of 60 x 60 metres, which seems extraordinarily small but is achievable if the men are in close order.[18] There might be any number of lines behind the first. Vegetius suggests six, although it seems unlikely that medieval troops waiting in the reserve lines would be sufficiently disciplined to resist joining in. Three feet per man would mean that 1,000 men would occupy a frontage of roughly 1,000 yards (just over 900 metres).

Heraldry

Heraldry was still important on the fifteenth-century battlefield. Banners and standards were used to identify units, and as rallying points in a mêlée. As battle was about to begin, the banners and standards were unfurled and displayed, and once the king was present on a battlefield with his standard and banners displayed, anyone in arms against him was committing treason. A banner was merely the coat of arms of the owner on a square or rectangular flag, while a standard showed the badge and motto of the owner and was much narrower than it was long. Some were enormous. The lengths of battle standards were officially laid down: that of a king was 8–9 yards long, and the size decreased with rank, down to 4 yards for a knight. The longer ones were supported on a small trolley since they were impossible to hold up, and these would usually have been used to indicate a command position, rather than be carried into battle. Heralds were usually still present on the battlefield, either to act as messengers, to negotiate surrender terms, or to make notes of what went on. We know that at least two of Richard's heralds were present. One carried his master's body from the battlefield on the back of his horse and the other was attainted.

Generalship

This was (and is) one of the most important aspects of warfare. Unless an army is commanded by a competent general, no amount of individual bravery can win a battle. Richard III was an experienced soldier. Although he had never commanded a large army in battle, he had been trusted with divisions of his brother's army at Barnet and Tewkesbury in 1471, acquitting himself well both times. He had also commanded the English army in the invasion of Scotland in 1482, which achieved the reconquest of Berwick and took Edinburgh, although no major battles were fought. Richard was thus used to handling large bodies of troops. There is no evidence that he took part in the popular noble sport of jousting; he obviously preferred real war, not play. He was interested in the chivalric code and gave the heralds their first corporate home in 1484, when he also made them a corporate body by charter. He was certainly a warlike character: he expressed the wish to Von Poppelau, a Bohemian visitor, that he could attack the Turks and drive them from Europe just using his Englishmen. There is thus no doubt that such a man should have had the ability to defeat Henry Tudor and his army. However, Tudor, who lacked any military experience himself, had in his army the Earl of Oxford, who was an experienced soldier and, as it turned out, a better general and tactician than the king.

Chapter 6

The Battle

Richard is said by the Crowland Chronicler and by Polydore Vergil to have spent a disturbed night before the battle, and suffered nightmare visions of all his so-called victims. That Richard did not sleep well is hardly surprising – not many men in his position would have done. He rose at daybreak (5.00 am on 22 August) or perhaps earlier, had his men roused and ordered divine service and breakfast for his men. But the Crowland Chronicler says neither Richard's breakfast nor divine service took place: 'At dawn on Monday morning the chaplains were not ready to celebrate mass for King Richard, nor was any breakfast ready to revive the king's flagging spirit.'[1] This is not the same as saying that mass was not heard at all, simply that the chaplains were not ready at the hour Richard got up.

However, there is some evidence for the absence of divine service from a much later manuscript concerning the miraculous effects caused by sight of the holy sacrament. It was written in about 1554 by Henry Parker, Lord Morley, who cites an account of one Bygoff or Bygot, a colleague of his in the household of the Countess of Richmond, mother of Henry Tudor. Bygot had formerly been in the households of Anne Neville and Richard III, and may have been Sir Ralph Bigot, a knight of the body and master of the king's ordnance. He was certainly present at Bosworth, where he was apparently injured. Bygot apparently said that the royal chaplains were unable to say mass before the battle because of what was apparently a complete lack of organisation. Bygot seems to have remained loyal to Richard III, his sworn lord, all his life, even while serving in the Tudor household, and so his testimony must bear some weight.[2]

However, even with this evidence, it seems most unlikely that Richard would have allowed his men to go into battle without hearing mass, nor, as a man of marked piety, would he have considered going into battle without hearing mass himself. It seems highly unlikely too, that his chaplains were so disorganised as to be unable to say divine service at all. It seems possible that whatever Bygot said, Parker exaggerated in order to emphasise how the miraculous effects of the holy sacrament were denied to the evil king, the result being that he lost the battle. There is in fact some evidence that plans had been made for divine service and the usual arrangements made. The fifteenth-century processional crucifix and staff found somewhere on the battlefield in the eighteenth century, where exactly is not known, are probably evidence that the king had with him a normal travelling royal chapel. This crucifix is exactly the kind of piece that would be expected as part of the equipment of such a travelling chapel.[3] There is a tradition that Richard heard his last mass in Sutton Cheney church, which is certainly possible if the royal camp lay near Sutton Cheney.

The Crowland Chronicler also says that Richard had a ghastly pale countenance because of the terrible night he had passed, and he told his men 'that whatever the outcome of [that] day's battle, to whichever side the victory was granted, would totally destroy the kingdom of England'. For he also declared that he would ruin all the partisans of the other side if he emerged the victor, predicting that his adversary would do exactly the same to the king's supporters if the victory fell to him. This depressing statement is amplified considerably by the Tudor chronicler Edward Hall,[4] who describes a further unsettling event for Richard that morning. He says that a verse was found pinned to the tent of the Duke of Norfolk, reading 'Jack of Norfolk be not too bold, For Dykon thy master is bought and sold' – in other words, that Richard had been, or was about to be, betrayed.[5] None of the other contemporary sources mentions this, although it was picked up by later writers, including Holinshed and Shakespeare, and it seems very likely that it is on a par with the speeches that Hall writes for Richard and Henry – i.e., invented – although it is possible that it represents an oral transmission of a fact. It seems reasonable to expect that both the Ballad of Lady Bessy and the Ballad of Bosworth Field would have included it if it was common knowledge.

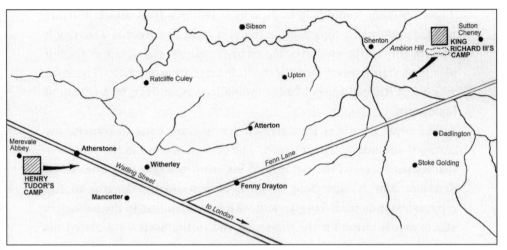

Map 2: Plan showing the area in which the battle was fought. (*Geoffrey Wheeler*)

The rival armies probably stirred at first light. Archaeological evidence suggests that the battle was fought on the plain south-west of Ambion Hill, which is what several later sources say, although the contemporary sources make no comment.[6] Therefore Richard would have led his army down from the hill towards Fenn Lane. Vergil, one of the earliest sources, says that there was a marsh between the two armies.[7] A marsh that was present in the fifteenth century has been located by the Battlefield Survey just south of Fenn Lane, at a place now known as Fenn Hole. It was probably not very large, although it was large enough to have been used to help defend a battle position. It thus seems likely that this is the marsh mentioned by Vergil. This conclusion is confirmed by the fact that the roundshot previously mentioned were nearly all found to the west of Fenn Hole, and fall into two distinct groups, together covering an area of roughly 1,000 by 1,500 yards (see map overleaf). These groups of shot would fit with two armies aligned roughly south/east to north/west with their flanks resting on the marsh; this tallies with Vergil, who says the marsh was between the armies and on the right flank of Tudor's army. The right flank of the royal army may have been resting on a small stream or extended across it, depending on the length and depth of the line.

These positions would help to prevent or inhibit a flank attack. Further proof that the battle took place in this area is the discovery of a silver gilt boar roughly on the ground occupied by the marsh, and a piece of the hilt of a high-status sword found a short distance from the boar. The boar, which was Richard's livery badge, would have been worn by a person of high status.

The royal army was thus arrayed across Fenn Lane to prevent any eastward advance by Tudor's men. The general opinion in the sources is that Richard arrayed the vanward of his army in a very long line. Vergil describes him as 'stretching it forth of a wonderful length, so full replenished both with footmen and with horsemen that to the beholders afar it gave a terror for the multitude and in the front were placed his

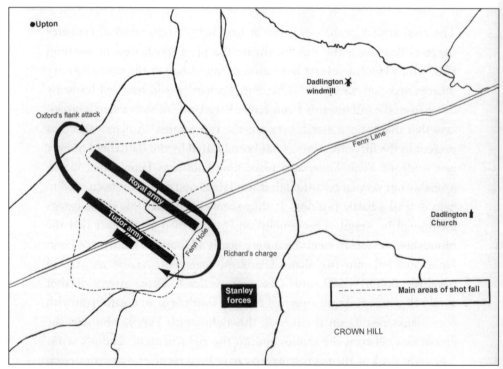

Map 3: The proposed site of the battle. (*Geoffrey Wheeler*)

archers, like a most strong trench and bulwark; of these archers he made leader John Duke of Norfolk'. By having a long line Richard was further endeavouring to prevent a flank attack, and also threatening the smaller rebel army with an enveloping operation to outflank them. To the rear of this long vanward 'followed the king himself with a choice force of soldiers'. The 'terrorising' aspect of the array must have been deliberate: Richard may have guessed that Tudor's troops were perhaps not very confident of success and such an overwhelming array would have made them (and their commander) even more anxious. In addition, Richard had put his most experienced soldier in command of this crucial position. Molinet says that Brackenbury was also posted with the vanward, and it may be that he was in command of the guns he had brought from the Tower. It is not clear if the horsemen mentioned by Vergil were acting as such, i.e., as cavalry, or were dismounted. Probably they were stationed on the wings, and may have been the scurriers that Vergil says were used at the start of the battle to prevent some of Richard's less enthusiastic troops from deserting. If Richard had positioned his scurriers as cavalry support on the wings, as was sometimes done, then they may well have had the effect Vergil describes, deliberately or not.[8] As the phrase 'choice force' implies, the men stationed with Richard in the rear may have been in the nature of elite cavalry, perhaps his household knights. There is no mention of the Earl of Northumberland's position in any of the sources, but a Spanish account by Diego de Valera says that 'Lord Tamorlant' commanded the left wing of the royal army and it seems very likely that Northumberland is meant. De Valera also says that the Great Chamberlain commanded the vanward: Norfolk, who did command the vanward, certainly did not hold this office but Northumberland did, and De Valera's informants must have confused the two.[9] It seems very likely that Northumberland was put in command of the left wing with his men as a further extension of the great line. Some authors have placed him at a distance from the main royal army in the rear but this seems highly unlikely, as he would have been little use, even potentially, at a distance from the main fighting. If the royal army was thus arrayed, then the line, based on the figures previously given for troop deployment and the size of the royal army (about 8,000 men), would have been perhaps 1,500 yards long, which would have taken it across the stream. A line 1,500 yards in length allows for the footmen to be five deep and for some horsemen to be deployed on the wings, whereas a line of about 1,000 yards, that is between the marsh and the stream, would enable a depth of perhaps eight men. Either would be a formidable sight. The guns were probably interspersed among the archers in the front lines.

Tudor was some 3 miles from Richard's chosen position at dawn on 22 August. Before setting out on his march he apparently asked Lord Stanley, who was already approaching the battle site, to take command of his van at the battle, but Stanley refused, commenting that since Henry's company was so small he would lend him four knights together 'with their chivalry' from his own forces to help him. The Ballad of Bosworth Field names them as Sir Robert Tunstall, Sir John Savage, Sir Hugh Persall and Sir Humphrey Stanley. Vergil says that early on the morning of 22 August Tudor sent to Lord Stanley, whose troops were approaching the battlefield, to come and join him, but that Stanley 'answered that the earl should set his own forces in order while he would come with his (own) army well appointed', and meanwhile Stanley settled his forces between the two armies. This reply was 'given contrary to what was looked for and to that which the opportunity of time and weight of cause required, though Henry were no little vexed and began to be somewhat appalled', as well he may have been. These two requests to Lord Stanley could be descriptions of the same event.[10]

Despite this setback, Tudor nevertheless now had no choice but to prepare for battle, so his men would have been roused, mustered into marching order and marched from Atherstone, a distance of about 3 miles from the royal army. This is no distance for fit men, especially those hardened by the long march from Milford Haven, and after two days' rest. At a marching speed of perhaps 2 miles an hour, to allow for poor roads, this would have taken them about an hour and a half. They were doubtless bringing their French guns but not their baggage train, which they could easily retrieve if they won and would not need if they lost. They might therefore have arrived on the battlefield at about 8.00 am. Tudor is said to have used local guides on this journey. William Burton, a local man writing in the seventeenth century, said that his ancestor John de Hardwick, lord of the nearby manor of Lindley and a commissioner of array for Leicestershire, joined Tudor on the day before the battle with men and horses, and served as a guide on the morning of the battle. Two other men in the rebel army, Sir Robert Harcourt and Sir John Cheyne, were also local and may have helped to guide Tudor's army.[11] With Tudor on the march were most of those prominent gentry and clergy who had fled to him in 1483. They included John, Lord Welles, Tudor's uncle, Edward Woodville, the queen's brother, and John Cheyne, as well as Piers Courtenay, Bishop of Exeter, and Robert Morton, who had been Master of the Rolls until 1483, when he joined the Buckingham rebellion. He was the nephew of John Morton, Bishop of Ely, who had played an active part in planning the invasion. Also present were Christopher Urswick and Richard Fox, who were to be prominent in the new Tudor administration.[12]

The route taken by Tudor to the battlefield may be traced by the payments he subsequently made to a number of villages because they sustained losses of corn and grains 'by us and our company at our late victorious field', much as he also recompensed Atherstone and the Abbot of Merevale for damage. Most of the compensation was given to the village of Witherley, which was perhaps in the direct route of the army, but Fenny Drayton received a good sum, with Mancetter and Atterton receiving less. Some of the damage may have been caused by troops foraging before the battle, or perhaps some of the rebel troops were quartered in these villages (although gathering them from such scattered locations might have been difficult in the event of a sudden attack). John Fox, the parson of Witherley, together with John Atherston, 'gentleman', were appointed to receive the money, and presumably to disburse it. At Witherley Tudor knighted more of his followers. These included William Brandon, who would not long enjoy his new status since he was shortly to die on the battlefield at the hands of King Richard.[13] By the time Tudor reached the battlefield, Richard must have been waiting for an hour or more. Once on the battlefield, Tudor 'made a slender vanward for the small number of his people; before the same he placed archers of whom he made captain John Earl of Oxford, in the right wing of the vanward he placed Gilbert Talbot to defend the same, in the left verily he set John Savage and himself, trusting to the aid of Thomas Stanley, with one troop of horsemen and a few footmen did follow'. The position described, with Talbot on the right of the vanward and Savage on the left, might indicate that the rebel army was arranged in the normal way with three battles, but it is more likely that there was in fact only one battle and that 'slender', with Oxford in overall command.[14]

The positions described here for the royal and rebel armies are typical of a medieval battle, but in this case there are some oddities. It may first of all be asked why Richard placed his army at such an odd angle across Fenn Lane. Had he wished to take up a more orthodox position he could have placed his army at right angles across Fenn Lane to prevent Tudor advancing any further east or trying to reach London. Had he wished, he could have positioned it so that the marsh protected his front, and he would then have been in a position to fire at Tudor as his army came in sight, elevating his guns to give them greater range. However, from the archaeological evidence to date, which consists of finds from a limited area, it appears that the armies were lined up in the way shown on the map (see p. 92). It may be that Richard chose this position because the Stanleys were already stationed on the slopes of Crown Hill when the royal army reached the battlefield, and he was trying to find a position for his army that could both counter any hostile movement from there and watch for the rebel advance. Vergil describes the battle preliminaries with both armies lined up opposite one another, and the positions described would correspond to his description that there was a 'marsh between both hosts, which Henry of purpose left on the right hand that it might serve his men instead of a fortress, by the doing thereof he left the sun on his back'. If the rebels did indeed reach the battlefield by 8.00 as suggested, the sun would probably have been sufficiently far advanced to be on their back by the time they lined up on the field, and there was certainly a marsh between the two hosts, albeit on one flank. According to Molinet, the armies were about a quarter of a league apart. If this was a French league, as seems likely from a French-speaking author, this would put the two sides about 800 yards apart. But this distance is well beyond bow shot (about 250 to 300 yards), the normal distance apart for opposing armies. If they were this distance apart, perhaps Tudor (or more likely Oxford, an experienced commander) was worried about the royal guns.[15]

It remains a matter for conjecture where the two Stanley brothers had placed themselves. Some authors have put them together but this seems unlikely since Sir William had already been declared a traitor and even at this stage Lord Stanley would have been reluctant to openly ally himself with the anti-Richard faction. Even though there was little the king could do about it at this late stage, it would have been much better to leave him (and Tudor too, of course) guessing about the intentions of both brothers. It therefore seems likely that Lord Stanley placed himself south of the main action, on Northumberland's flank, perhaps on the slope of Crown Hill from where he could see what was happening. There was no action at all on this part of the battle line, the Crowland Chronicler specifically stating that 'Where the Earl of Northumberland stood, however, with a fairly large and well equipped force, there was no contest against the enemy and no blows given or received in battle'. This was not the fault of Northumberland; if he were not directly attacked, then he could not break the line without a general advance of the royal army, which did not take place. Presumably Richard, half expecting Stanley to attempt a flank attack, had to guard against such a move, hence the positioning of a valuable part of his army there. Sir William Stanley, who did intervene in the battle, may have been lower down on the slope of the hill to the west of his brother, and nearer Tudor's forces.[16]

Even before the fighting started – indeed, while the rebel army was still moving into position according to the Crowland Chronicler – it must have become obvious that Lord Stanley was probably against the king rather than for him, and so the king apparently ordered the execution of Lord Strange. The chronicler then says, 'However, those to whom the task was given, seeing that the matter in hand was at a very critical stage and that it was more important than the elimination of one man, failed to carry out that king's cruel command and on their own judgement let the man go and returned to the heart of the battle.' The ballads agree that Strange was not executed because of lack of time, and both describe the whole scene at length in a most affecting way, and even suggest that Strange was given time to send a message to his wife. That such a minor detail is mentioned at all is perhaps an indication of the truth of the matter as a whole, since it would have been a memorable enough event. That Strange was not executed because of a shortage of time to carry out the order seems unlikely, and perhaps shows that the order was never given in the first place. Both the ballads say that Richard could see Lord Stanley's banner, which could legitimately have been interpreted as the taking up of arms against his sovereign – that is, he was committing a treasonable act. This is perhaps the implication of the words in the Ballad of Bosworth Field: 'I see the banner of Lord Stanley he said, Fetch hither the Lord Strange to me, for doubtless he shall die this day'.[17]

As soon as the men of both armies saw the opposing forces, they put on their helmets and generally readied themselves for battle. Vergil says that as soon as the king saw the enemy forces pass the marsh, he ordered his men to commence the battle, which they did, with 'great shouts'. The king ordered his artillery and also his archers to fire, and the rebels replied, certainly with arrows and we now know with guns too, although there is no reference in the sources to guns being fired by the rebel army.[18]

During the rebel advance the French chronicler Molinet says that the royal army fired on the Tudor troops as soon as they came within range. Perhaps the king had positioned some of his guns to fire to the flank. Molinet goes on to say that 'the French, knowing by the king's shot the lie of the land and the order of his battle resolved in order to avoid the fire to mass their troops against the flank rather than the front of the king's battle'.[19] Oxford and the other commanders (the French ones, according to Molinet) would have seen that the royal army was larger than their own and the obvious danger was that they could be overwhelmed by sheer numbers. They could not rely on a Stanley intervention, so a new strategy was urgently needed. From what Molinet says, it appears that the rebels eventually launched a flank attack, although the archaeological evidence in the form of shot found on the royal position suggests that at least part of the Tudor army was ranged in front of the royal army. The fact that a large part of the rebel army was massed on one flank could have been masked by the guns and a large part of the archer contingent. It may be wondered why, if the king was already in position when the rebel army came within sight of the battlefield, the rebels did not immediately make an attack on the flank, taking advantage of the fact that the king's guns were probably mostly sited facing the front and were difficult to move at short notice. A flank advance and attack would have had the element of surprise and would have been a difficult tactic to counter; it would also largely negate the king's numerical superiority in artillery and men, since he could not bring his whole force to bear against the enemy.

Nevertheless, a short way into the battle Oxford put his plan into operation, ordering that 'in every rank that no soldier should go above ten feet from the standards; which charge being known, when all men had thronged together and stayed awhile from fighting the adversaries were therewith afraid supposing some fraud and so they all forebore the fight a certain space'. The rebels were thus ordered to go into close order and while doing this the fighting slackened. It may well be that the royal army was wary of a trap. The Earl of Oxford then put his men into 'array triangle' (that is, in a wedge), and vigorously renewed the fight.[20] This wedge formation was employed on the continent, where the flanks of the wedge were protected by pikemen, and so we can assume that many of the French mercenaries in the rebel army were pikemen. Such troops and formations were unfamiliar to English soldiers, and the terrifying psychological effect as the point of the wedge advanced boldly out of the left flank of the rebel army with the tall pikes sticking up like a massive hedgehog can be imagined.[21] It is very likely that the gunners and the archers in the remaining part of Tudor's army provided such covering fire as they could. This attack was a success, according to Vergil.

Richard had probably thought that when it came to actual combat his troops would be more than a match for the rebel army, but it seems the rebels fought better and they certainly used tactics that surprised the king. That the rebel army fought so well may be at least partly due to the fact that on their long march to Bosworth the different groups of soldiers had had time to get used to one another and their commanders, and had settled down into a cohesive force. It seems much more likely to be related to the fact that most of the troops in the rebel army were professional French and Scottish soldiers. If, as suggested, these foreign troops were indeed using the long pikes now common on continental battlefields, then the English troops would have had little or no idea of how to cope with them. Certainly Richard's men did not have any time to come together into an army. Troops that were hastily recruited, not all well equipped and generally inexperienced would hardly have been an expert force. This would not have mattered so much had they been facing a similar group of men. Unfortunately for the king, they were not.[22] This was dangerous for the king, because if the rebels seemed to be winning then his own men might start to panic and flee.

At some point in the hard fighting the Duke of Norfolk was killed (by Sir John Savage, according to the Ballad of Lady Bessy), perhaps while trying to rally his men. After this, the royal army's vanguard started to collapse. Again according to the Ballad of Lady Bessy, Norfolk was killed near a windmill while fleeing with his troops. The Dadlington windmill was well over 1,000 yards from the main action, so if Norfolk was killed there it must certainly have been during a rout. No other source suggests that Norfolk was killed anywhere but in the battle. A livery badge of an eagle was discovered near the mill, so there may well have been some military action here.[23] It seems probable, though, that Norfolk was killed in the battle. Richard, seeing this, feared that Norfolk's death would cause a collapse of morale and thus decided that he should try to bring the battle to an end at a stroke. As Vergil says: 'King Richard understood, first by espialls [observation] where Earl Henry was far off with a small force of soldiers about him, then after drawing nearer he knew it perfectly by evident signs and tokens that it was Henry, wherefore all inflamed with ire he struck his horse with spurs and runneth out of the one side without the vanwards against him', probably charging right round Northumberland's right wing and avoiding the marsh. Richard may have hoped that Northumberland would join him. It must have been a dramatic sight as the king galloped from the side of his army towards Tudor with his troop of horsemen and a 'few footmen'.[24] This elite body of men, formed from the royal household and bodyguard, would have numbered several hundred armed and mounted men. If the king's 'espials' had shown him that Tudor was bearing the undifferenced royal arms to show his pretensions, this might account for a large part of his anger.

A charge such as the one Richard undertook was not an unknown tactic in late fifteenth-century warfare, and had it worked, it would have put an end to the battle at a stroke. The rebel army would not have stood firm if their leader had fled or been killed. Vergil says that Tudor saw King Richard coming at him but because at that stage he could do nothing but fight, he received the king with great determination. Richard overthrew Tudor's standard (the 'royal' standard), together with Sir William Brandon, the standard-bearer, and beat to the ground Sir John Cheyne, a man of great height and strength. Vergil then goes on to say that Richard 'made way with weapons on every side'. Henry 'abode the brunt far longer than ever his own soldiers would have thought possible who were now almost out of hope of victory', as indeed Tudor himself probably was. It seems likely that the French troops played a significant part in defending Tudor, and his footmen may well have been some of the French pikemen fighting in the continental style, although evidently there were not enough of them to form a proper defensive square to repel horsemen since Richard and at least some of his men broke through and came close enough to Tudor to kill his standard bearer, who would have been very close to him. Information on the part played by the French mercenaries comes from a letter written by one of them on the day after the battle. Only a small part of this letter is known, and in it Richard is quoted as saying, 'These French traitors are today the cause of our realm's ruin.' The letter also says that Tudor was protected on foot in the middle of the mercenaries, presumably within the partial pike square.[25]

The mercenaries sent by Charles VIII of France therefore seem to have played an essential part in helping to hold off Richard's attack until the Stanleys finally took action. It seems Sir William Stanley decided at last that the time had come to join the battle. Unfortunately for the king, he chose Tudor's side, and 'he came betime unto our king' as the Ballad of Bosworth Field has it.[26] The muddled Castilian Report has Richard being killed while fighting the troops of the Lord Tamorlant, who had been in charge of Richard's left wing but had turned against his lord. As we have seen, it is most likely that Tamorlant is a mistake for the Earl of Northumberland, who was indeed on Richard's left wing. It seems probable here that he has been mistaken for one of the Stanleys, who were both separately on Richard's left and could conceivably have been mistakenly described as the king's left wing. It has been ingeniously argued by Oliver Harris that Sir William, who had no real reason to support Tudor, unlike his brother who was married to Tudor's mother, had intended to intervene on the side of the king, but because both Tudor and the king were bearing the undifferenced royal arms the wrong bearer of the royal arms was killed in the heat of the battle.[27] This may be unlikely, but Harris goes on to suggest that Tudor may have suspected this is what had happened, since Sir William did not receive the rewards that he might have expected for his action. The lack of reward might also have been caused, as was said by Lord Bacon in his life of Henry VII, by the fact that although Sir William arrived in time to save his life in the battle, Tudor must have been all too aware that he had stayed his hand quite long enough to endanger it.[28]

The report given by Vergil was that Richard 'could have saved himself by flight', and this is repeated by Diego de Valera, who says that Juan de Salazar, who was present at Richard's side during the battle, saw the treason being committed and urged the king to flee in order to fight again another day. De Valera goes on to say that at this point Richard put his royal crown over his helmet, donned his surcoat with the royal coat of arms and fought valiantly for a long time, heartening those who remained loyal and upholding the battle himself. The ballads repeat this, saying that an unnamed knight told Richard that his horse was at hand and he could with honour retreat and fight again another day. All sources except one agree that Richard died like a king, saying that when he was urged to fly he said fiercely that he would win or die that day as king. Vergil says that he 'alone was killed fighting manfully in the thickest press of his enemies'. Even the Crowland Chronicler, who was no friend to Richard, agrees. The exception is Molinet, who claims that Richard tried to flee and was killed when his horse became mired in the marsh. This seems unlikely if the suggestions given here are correct for the relative positions of the armies and the point where the struggle with Tudor took place. Only Molinet suggests that Richard died in the marsh; tellingly the eye-witness Spanish account does not, and nor do the ballads. Such a scene would have presented a marvellous opportunity for a ballad maker. Who dealt the fatal blow is not known, and certainly no one was rewarded afterwards for doing so. Molinet, rather than claiming that it was a Frenchman, as might have been expected, in fact says that it was a Welsh halberdier. It was claimed afterwards on behalf of Rhys ap Thomas that he had killed Richard, although he was certainly not a Welsh halberdier. The family of Ralph Rudyard, from Rudyard near Leek in Staffordshire, also claimed afterwards that he had killed Richard.[29]

However Richard met his end, he was the only English king to die in battle. According to the proclamation issued by Henry afterwards, he died at Sandford.[30] The fighting was then over in a matter of minutes as the royal army broke ranks and fled. As described, Oxford was already getting the better of the van after much hard fighting. The death of Norfolk would further have disheartened the royal troops, and great numbers of them are said to have thrown away their weapons with relief and submitted themselves to Henry, the new king. Most of the sources say that many of the royal troops were there reluctantly and were pleased to stop fighting. That many of the levies were reluctant is a reasonable comment but the implication in the sources is that men did not want to fight for Richard and would have fled sooner if they could have done so. That at least some members of Richard's army did not apparently want to fight for him is shown by the petition of Roger Wake of Blisworth, Northants, against his attainder on the grounds that it was against his 'will and mind' to fight for King Richard (rather implausibly, as Cavill says, since he was Catesby's brother-in-law). He also appealed on the grounds that he had a wife and eight children who were too young to be able to support themselves, and that it was contrary to his wife's upbringing to apply for alms. Another who appealed against his attainder was Geoffrey St German, who had died the day after Bosworth, perhaps due to wounds received in the fighting. His daughter and heir said that he was only with the royal army because he was 'so threatened by the same late duke's [i.e., Richard III's] letters that unless he came to the same field he should lose his life, lands and goods, that for dread of the same he was most unwillingly at the same field'. Quite why St German should have been attainted is unclear: he was only a minor land-holder of Broughton in Northants (although he had been one of those asked by Richard for a loan, so he must have been thought of by Richard or his advisers as a supporter). Wake was more prominent, having been Sheriff of Northants.[31] Another odd aspect of the whole matter is that the words of Richard's letter that so alarmed St German were the standard words used in any royal command, such as a commission of array, at this time. Wake used the same argument as part of his appeal. Both men, and everyone else, must have been well aware that these words were always used.

As the royal army began to flee, Northumberland and his troops were probably still standing firm in their position on the left wing of the royal army. Molinet says Northumberland should have charged the French (as he consistently describes Tudor's army), but in fact he did nothing except flee because he had an understanding with Tudor. Northumberland was arrested after the battle but we do not know if this happened on the battlefield. He was released fairly quickly, certainly by early December, although he was not summoned to Parliament in September.[32] As well as the Duke of Norfolk, Walter, Lord Ferrers, Sir Richard Ratcliffe, Sir Robert Percy (controller of the royal household), Sir Robert Brackenbury (Constable of the Tower), John Kendall, Richard's secretary, and many others were killed. Lord Lovell fled east, because he is next heard of in sanctuary at Colchester, together with Humphrey and Thomas Stafford. The Earl of Surrey, son of the Duke of Norfolk, was arrested and attainted, but was released in 1489 and restored to his earldom. Vergil says 1,000 of the king's troops died but only about 100 of Tudor's. These figures may be correct as far as the royal army is concerned, but are certainly too low for Tudor's army. The battle may have been over by mid-morning. Vergil says that it lasted more than two hours but we do not know exactly when it started.[33]

It is unclear in which direction the royal troops fled. It seems logical that they would flee north-east, towards Sutton Cheney and away from the enemy, and it seems very unlikely that the majority would flee southwards right through the victorious army. That some at least fled towards Sutton Cheney may be indicated by the discovery of the eagle livery badge at Dadlington mill. However, that some fled south could be shown by the apparently fifteenth-century burials found in and around the churchyard at Dadlington. Here a chantry chapel was set up in 1511 by Henry VIII to pray for the souls of those killed at the battle, and there is evidence that at least some of the battlefield dead had been transferred to Dadlington churchyard by this date. It is possible that the bones were brought here from where they were originally buried, as sometimes happened when a battlefield chantry was set up, as at Towton. No large burial pits have been found. There are various records of finds of bones and armour at various times in the seventeenth and late eighteenth centuries, but it is unclear where many of these were found. One of them appears to have been near Whitemoors, just under a mile south of Shenton, and another, apparently of armour only, was north of Ambion Hill.[34]

While the slaughter of the beaten and fleeing royal army was still taking place, Henry Tudor was busy giving thanks to God for his victory. Then, 'replenished with joy incredible', he took himself to the nearest hill and commended his soldiers before ordering the wounded to be looked after and the dead to be buried. Bernard Andre, Henry's French poet laureate, writing much later in his reign, says that Henry ordered the dead to be given 'honourable burial', and goes on to say that 'King Richard himself should be buried with all reverence'.[35] Henry then thanked the nobles and commanders with him and knighted some of them, including Gilbert Talbot, who had brought the Talbot levies, Rhys ap Thomas, who had brought Welsh troops, and Humphrey Stanley, a distant cousin of Lord Stanley, while all present cried 'God save King Henry'. He was then crowned with Richard's crown – that is, the coronet from Richard's helmet (but see Appendix 4) – by Thomas Stanley. Traditionally he is said to have been crowned on the hill now known as Crown Hill, on the slopes of which the Stanleys were probably stationed. The crown is traditionally said to have been found in a thorn bush, where it had rolled when Richard was finally struck down. It may have been hidden there by a looter for later retrieval, and certainly Vergil says it was found among the spoils. The amount of plundered goods available in the markets of London after the battle must have been immense.[36] The new king ordered the baggage to be packed up and set off in the evening for Leicester, which he entered wearing his new crown. The procession was accompanied by the naked body of the late king, treated with insufficient humanity, according to the Crowland Chronicler, and a 'miserable spectacle in good sooth', on the back of a horse with a rope around his neck and with his arms and legs hanging down. He may have been on the horse of one of his Pursuivants, Blanc Sanglier Pursuivant.[37] It is unfortunate that because Richard lost the battle his heralds were not in a position to write an account of it afterwards, as they did of the next battle, at Stoke, in 1487.

The late king's body was exposed to public view for two days to prove that Richard was dead, and was then buried with little ceremony. Vergil says that the body was exposed in the church of the Grey Friars but the later ballads say that it was exposed in the Newark (an area of Leicester), perhaps in the Lancastrian foundation of the Annunciation of Our Lady. Wherever the body was exposed, there is now no doubt that it was buried in the Grey Friars' church, in the choir as Rous said, a place of honour. A tomb was later erected by the order of Henry VII, but there is no description of it except that it may have been made of 'mingle coloured marble' (that is, alabaster) and probably had an inscribed effigy of the king on the top. The tomb was destroyed during the Reformation. All trace of the grave had vanished until it was revealed in 2012 during excavations in Leicester.[38] See also Appendix 6, Epilogue.

The signature of Henry VII. (*Geoffrey Wheeler*)

Chapter 7

After the Battle

Henry Tudor, now King Henry VII, spent two days in Leicester while essential business was transacted. This doubtless included fending off all those who now claimed their reward from the new king and sending the foreign mercenaries back home. Henry was in a rather strange position. He had been brought up in Wales, had been in exile for fourteen years and had only been in England once in his life before he came to Bosworth. This was in 1470 when, according to later Tudor historians, he was presented to Henry VI, who predicted that he would later become king.[1] He knew none of the surviving members of the old regime, and they did not know him. He lacked experience in administration, having no knowledge of how the royal household functioned. The centre of the household administration, Richard's secretary John Kendall, had died in the battle, although there must have been many more junior clerks left behind in Leicester. One of the major problems faced by Henry at the beginning of his reign was precisely that he did not know the people on whom he would have to rely. To a great extent the appointments he made in the early part of his reign were chosen from people he knew, especially those who had been in exile with him, and they largely stayed with him throughout his reign. A significant lack of official business was transacted before early September, so it obviously took a few weeks to get the government machine started up again.[2]

Some business, however, could not wait. William Catesby, Richard's Chancellor and Chamberlain of the Exchequer, was taken into custody after the battle. He had been a central figure in the old administration and it might have been thought that Henry would want to make use of his expertise but apparently not, because Catesby was executed three days after the battle. It has been suggested that this was to calm the animosity roused by Catesby's acquisition of estates in the Leicestershire area, but it seems unlikely that a man as cautious as Henry Tudor would remove a potentially useful man for this reason. It may be that Catesby had simply made too many enemies among the victors. Whatever the reason, he made his will on 25 August, probably in some haste. He asked that his debts be paid and appointed 'his dear and well beloved wife to whom I have ever been true of my body' his executrix. He 'doubts not that the king will be a good and gracious lord [to his wife and children] for he is called a full gracious prince and I never offended him by my good and free will for God I take to my judge I have ever loved him'. Catesby seems to have felt betrayed by the Stanleys, and asked that they 'help and pray for my soul as you have not for my body as I trusted in you'. It would be very interesting to know precisely what lies behind this statement.[3] The only other executions that took place were those of William Bracher, a Yeoman of the Crown and a commissioner of array for Somerset, and his son. Both were hanged.[4] That there were no more executions seems to show that Henry had indeed determined on a policy of clemency, as he had said in the official proclamation announcing his accession. Even the number of attainders passed in Henry's first Parliament was not high in the circumstances.

Whatever else was going on in Leicester, the new king wasted no time in sending out the proclamations announcing his accession and the speed with which this was done is shown by the example of the city of York, which received Henry's proclamation on 24 August. In fact, the news had reached York by 23 August, the day after the battle, when John Spooner, sergeant of the mace, returned to his city. He had remained with Richard after having been sent with a colleague to discover what troops they should send. He may have fought at Bosworth, or waited in Leicester for news, but he must certainly have left for York as soon as he knew the result of the battle and must have galloped at breakneck speed to bring the news to the city council so quickly. The news was recorded in the council minute book in heartfelt terms: 'that King Richard, late mercifully reigning upon us, was through great treason of the Duke of Norfolk and

The brass of William Catesby, d.1485. (*Geoffrey Wheeler*)

many others that turned against him, with many other lords and nobles of this north parts was piteously slain and murdered to the great heaviness of this city'. Under a new king, this was very close to treasonable. This was entered in the minute book as being made on 23 August, 'anno etc, *vacat regalis partas*' ('the throne is vacant'). The York authorities did not record a regnal year until 27 August (and occasionally did not do so after that) but dated by the calendar year only. Another note recorded in the minutes, perhaps by John Spooner himself, and dated 22 August says that the 'the lord king' was killed at Sandferth beside Leicester', together with John, Duke of Norfolk, Thomas (*sic*), Earl of Lincoln, Thomas, Earl of Surrey, 'son of the aforesaid duke', Francis, Viscount Lovell, Lord Walter Devereux, Lord Ferrers, Sir Richard Ratcliffe 'and many other knights, squires and gentlemen'. The names of Surrey, Lincoln and Lovell were later deleted, presumably when more accurate information about survivors became available. Interestingly, this is the first reference to Sandford as the place where Richard died.[5]

The news reached York officially on 24 August in the form of a message borne by Sir Roger Cotam, 'knight unto the king's grace come to this city to proclaim the said King Henry'. Unfortunately for Sir Roger, it appears that he dared not come into the city for fear of death – perhaps a sign of the depth of feeling for the late king in York – so the mayor and aldermen went to see him at a tavern called the Boar. This may have been a significant choice of venue since the badge of Richard III was a white boar. Sir Roger showed the civic authorities the proclamation of Henry naming him as king and saying that he would be as good and gracious a lord as any of his predecessors had been. On the next day, 25 August, Windsor Herald (Richard Slack), who had presumably accompanied Cotam, was received in the council chamber wearing 'upon him a coat armour of the arms of England and France'. Windsor handed the mayor a proclamation from the king and told him to proclaim it throughout the city. This proclamation was given in the name of 'Henry by the grace of God, King of England and of France, prince of Wales and lord of Ireland' and ordered that men should keep the peace and not carry out private quarrels on pain of hanging. This last part was obviously an attempt to prevent the private exaction of revenge or the settling of old scores by either side. It further stated that 'Richard Duke of Gloucester, late called King Richard, was slain at a place called Sandford, within the shire of Leicester and brought dead off the field unto the town of Leicester and there was laid openly that every man might see and look upon him', and went on to list those killed with him, who again included the Earl of Lincoln, Viscount Lovell and the Earl of Surrey. It must have been very swiftly known to the king that these men had not died, and it has been suggested that their names were deliberately included here in an attempt to prevent men rallying round them.[6]

Windsor Herald and presumably Sir Roger Cotam probably went on to proclaim the new king throughout the north east, and if the duties were as hazardous as they appear to have been in York then Windsor Herald certainly merited his reward of £20 on 14 October 1485 for 'certain special considerations'. Henry also later paid for his wedding garments. Cotam, probably in fact Coton, was also well rewarded, being made Sheriff of Glamorgan and Morgannock on 22 September 1485.[7] The use of at least one herald for this purpose is interesting. The Yorkist kings did use heralds in this way but they became much more prominent in Henry's reign, rather as if both sides saw that this would be to their advantage, the heralds not least because they might have thought that their closeness to Richard III made it important for them to show that they could work for the new king too.[8]

Another important piece of business early in Henry's reign was for him to get into his own hands Edward, Earl of Warwick, son of the late Duke of Clarence; as the last male Plantagenet, he was a potential focus for rebellion. Henry accordingly sent Sir Robert Willoughby north to Sheriff Hutton, where Edward was living. He was duly given into Sir Robert's custody and delivered to the Tower of London, where he lived for the rest of his life. Elizabeth, the eldest daughter of Edward IV, whom Henry had promised to marry, was probably also in Sheriff Hutton and she was escorted to London in the company of 'noble ladies' and sent to stay with her mother.[9]

Henry probably left Leicester on 24 or 25 August, and made his way to London. He did not hurry: indeed, he was probably relishing the attention he received along the way and the relief of no longer being a wanted man. According to Vergil, he made his way like a triumphing general and was greeted everywhere by cheering crowds. He entered London on 3 September, to an even more triumphant welcome. The mayor and corporation, who had already paid their respects to the king, met him at Hornsey, and the mayor and aldermen in scarlet robes and the citizens in violet escorted the new king into London with much celebration and the reading of some verses by Henry's blind poet laureate, Bernard Andre. Henry was taken to the north door of St Paul's cathedral, where at the Rood he offered up the three banners he had flown at Bosworth, one displaying St George, one a Welsh red dragon and one the dun cow on yellow tartan. A Te Deum then took place in the cathedral and Henry retired to the palace of the Bishop of London.[10]

The real business of governing the country now began. As early as 30 August, while Henry was still on his way to London, his household staff took delivery of a very large quantity of material from which to make new clothing, some for the king and some for his servants, the cost of which was over £358. This had already been paid for by Sir Reginald Bray, soon to be Chancellor of the Duchy of Lancaster, and a man who continued to be of central importance to the Tudor regime.[11]

Some of the earliest business involved making appointments and handing out rewards, not only to Henry's leading supporters but also to many of the more humble men who had gathered round him in France or had joined his banner on his march through Wales and England. Henry took great care to repay debts of gratitude for support in this way. It was decided very quickly to hold the coronation on 30 October, which gave the staff of the royal wardrobe rather longer to prepare than they had had for the previous coronation, that of Richard III. Jasper Tudor, Henry's uncle, received his due reward for his work on behalf of his nephew, being made Duke of Bedford three days before the coronation. Without his support, it is unlikely that Henry's invasion would have taken place at all. He was also found a wife in the person of Catherine Woodville, widow of the Duke of Buckingham. Thomas Stanley was promoted to Earl of Derby on the same day, while Edward Courtenay had been created Earl of Devon the day before. Sir William Stanley was given valuable offices but not a peerage, which he might have expected to receive, given that he had come to the new king's rescue at Bosworth. The coronation was splendidly arranged, but of course the organisers had the advantage of having had the recent coronation of Richard III to use as a model.[12]

Parliament was summoned to meet not long after the coronation, on 7 November. It was important for Henry to be crowned first and then to be recognised as king in Parliament in his own right. He could not afford for it to appear that any part of his claim to the throne was due to Elizabeth of York, and he did not marry her until January. The delay was caused in large part by the fact that until the act *Titulus Regius* of Richard III was reversed in Parliament, Elizabeth was illegitimate and Henry could not be seen to marry a bastard, but the other reason for the delay must have been due to the fact that a papal dispensation was needed, since Elizabeth and Henry were related in the fourth degree of kinship and affinity. It took time for dispensations to be sought and granted. In Henry's first Parliament the title of the king was duly rehearsed. He based it on the fact that he was *de facto* king, which one supposes was how he had been able to call a Parliament in the first place. The fact that he was under attainder was ignored. In his speech to Parliament Henry emphasised both his hereditary right to the throne and the fact that he was king by the judgement of God at Bosworth.[13] An act of attainder was passed against Richard, 'late Duke of Gloucester calling and naming himself by usurpation King Richard III', and 28 of his supporters including the Duke of Norfolk, the Earl of Surrey, 3 other peers, 8 knights, including Robert Brackenbury and Richard Ratcliffe, and 15 others, including John Kendall and William Catesby. The number of attainders is relatively low, perhaps because of Henry's need to win support, but there were some notable figures among those not attainted. For example, Richard's heir John, Earl of Lincoln, who was almost certainly at the battle and was probably one of the captives, was not attainted. His father the Duke of Suffolk may have spoken for him, but it might have been expected that

Lincoln was beyond pardon at this moment. The list of men attainted is a roll call of many of the leading supporters of Richard's regime, and it is interesting that as well as his prominent northern supporters, such as the two Harringtons, there are several southerners. Some who were not named, such as Sir Robert Percy, were from the north, and it seems likely that there were at least as many northerners in Richard's army as those from elsewhere. Of course, some of Richard's northern supporters may well have been in the army of the Earl of Northumberland. There were some fairly minor men in the list of those attainted, and it is difficult to understand why they should have been included. In some cases it may be that there was an element of score settling by those advising on the names.

Henry's act of attainder dated his reign from 21 August – the day before the battle of Bosworth – which meant that men who had fought in good faith for King Richard, the reigning monarch, were *de facto* made into traitors. As seen above, Henry had already called himself king before he reached Bosworth, and his action in Parliament was a dubious piece of sharp practice that the commons were very uneasy about. If this could be done once, it could be done again, and the risk would make men reluctant to fight for the king if they could be made into traitors by a later stroke of a pen. A contemporary letter says: 'there was many gentlemen against it, but it would not be, for it was the king's pleasure', and Henry stood firm on this matter and it was only ten years later that he agreed to allow an act that in effect outlawed this practice. The last piece of business was a petition from the commons for Henry to marry Elizabeth of York. This he graciously agreed to do. This first session of Parliament was prorogued on 10 December until 23 January the following year.[14]

The wedding was finally celebrated on 18 January 1486, a little more than three years since Henry had sworn to marry Elizabeth in Rennes cathedral. After the wedding Henry set off for a progress to the north. This was a part of the country that he really needed to make sure was, if not wholly loyal, at least not about to erupt in rebellion. He could not take overt action against the many families who had supported Richard, because apart from any other consideration he did not have the military power to do so. He had already issued a proclamation on 11 October publicising his willingness to give pardons to all the knights and gentry in the counties of Nottinghamshire, Yorkshire, Durham, Westmorland and Cumberland as well as in the city of York and the bishopric of Durham who had been in arms against him 'in the field' for all offences committed against him before 22 September of that year. The only exceptions were Sir Richard Ratcliffe, Sir James and Sir Robert Harington, Sir Thomas Pilkington, Sir Thomas Broughton, Sir Robert Middleton, and Thomas and Miles Metcalf. All except Broughton and the Metcalfs had already been attainted. Henry must have hoped that this pardon would effectively quieten those counties, although on 15 October he had to ask the Stanleys (including Sir Edward Stanley, now Sheriff of Lancashire) to raise the levies of their area because he had heard that the Scots were planning an invasion and it seemed likely that they would be helped by disaffected Yorkists in the north. By 20 October he had ordered them to stand down the levies, since his pardon had caused the rebels to disperse. The Scottish invasion failed to materialise.

However, things were still unsettled in the north when Henry set off on his progress in March 1486, and it was apparent that the disturbances were likely to continue.[15] He moved slowly north, stopping for Easter in Lincoln, where he worshipped in the cathedral. As he made his way towards York he learned of a planned uprising led by Viscount Lovell and Humphrey Stafford, who had both escaped from sanctuary. In fact it seems probable that he had been aware of this plot before he left London, because not only did he take with him his recently instituted bodyguard of the Yeoman of the (King's) Guard but he also seems to have arranged for the augmentation of his forces as he moved towards York. At Pontefract he was joined by a large part of the peerage, including the Earls of Lincoln, Oxford, Shrewsbury, Rivers and Wiltshire. In York itself he was received with very similar ceremonies to those used to welcome Richard III three years earlier, and the king in turn put on a display of great magnificence to demonstrate his kingly qualities.[16]

While Henry was in York rumours spread that a large number of rebels had gathered around Middleham and Richmond, the old lordships of Richard III, and were intending to march on York. Henry was not at first concerned, according to Vergil, but when he learned from his own servants that there was indeed an uprising, 'he was struck by great fear'. However, the rebellion was not supported as well as its leaders had hoped it would be, and when Henry sent the forces at his disposal against them they dispersed and the leaders fled. Henry had survived his first challenge, and must have moved slowly back southwards with great relief. On 20 September his first child, a son named Arthur, was born in Winchester.[17]

The abortive rising of 1486 was only a foretaste of a much more dangerous one in 1487. This time the rebels were led by Lord Lovell and also by the Earl of Lincoln, who had now thrown in his lot with the Yorkist faction. The rebels had at their head a pretender calling himself the Earl of Warwick, although the real Warwick was still in the Tower of London. The pretender had been crowned Edward VI in Dublin cathedral, and the rebel army included a substantial force of 3,500 mercenaries commanded by Martin Schwarz, a highly regarded Swiss captain, as well as many poorly armed Irishmen. In June the rebel army landed in Lancashire and marched into England. Henry gathered troops against them and on 16 June Lincoln and Lovell, with a force of about 8,000 men, including the mercenaries and the Irish troops, plus some English troops who had joined them, met Henry's larger army at Stoke, near Nottingham. Henry's army was led again by Oxford. The Yorkists were heavily defeated, and Lincoln, Schwarz and probably Lovell were all killed. This battle can reasonably be called the last one of the Wars of the Roses, and after it Henry was at last secure on the throne, although for the rest of his life he was never sure of this.[18]

Appendix 1

The Sources for the Battle

As far as possible in this book contemporary sources for events are used, although chronicles written in the mid-sixteenth century are also noted where what they say could be true or are corroborated by something earlier. As already mentioned, the battle of Bosworth is relatively well documented for a medieval battle and the major sources are discussed here in order of importance.

(a) The first is Polydore Vergil's *Anglica Historia* ('History of England'). The version used in this book is the sixteenth-century translation edited by Henry Ellis (1844). Vergil was a priest of international reputation as a humanist before he came to England in 1502 as the deputy of his patron Cardinal Adriano Castelli, as a collector of papal taxes. Vergil lived in England for most of the rest of his life, although he died in Italy in 1555. He claimed to have been commissioned by Henry VII to write the *History of England*, and this may be true since although he did not receive any major rewards in patronage from Henry, he did enjoy a steady stream of lesser awards. Vergil wrote the portion of the work covering the reign of Richard III no later than 1513 and probably earlier. He thus wrote his book some 25 years after the event and he certainly incorporates information from eye-witnesses, both to the battle itself and to the events leading up to it. He may have spoken to the Earl of Surrey, for example, one of Richard's commanders and the son of the Duke of Norfolk. Vergil shows an unusually keen interest in describing military events, and may have asked veterans of Bosworth to explain the tactics used in the battle. His description of military matters, such as the formation and deployment of the vanwards, has echoes of the Roman military textbook by Vegetius, *De Re Militari*, which was much used in the Middle Ages. His description seems to show a 'degree of professional expertise in captains and soldiers' that is not hinted at in accounts of other battles.[1]

Vergil claimed he was telling the truth, and this is probably correct within the limits of being tactful about the dead ancestors of powerful men and the need to put a favourable interpretation on the rise of the new dynasty. Nevertheless he is important as a major source for the whole reign of Richard III, as well as for the battle of Bosworth, and his work seems generally to be factually accurate. He must have spoken to many people who had been active in high places in Richard's reign. His bias against Richard was confined to the attribution of evil motives for his actions, and we have no reason to think that Vergil did not believe that these were Richard's motives.[2]

(b) The Crowland Chronicle was probably written in 1486, perhaps in April. The identity of the author has been the subject of much discussion: he was certainly a churchman and he must have been in the inner circles of the royal government, possibly the innermost, if he was indeed John Russell, Bishop of Lincoln and Richard's Chancellor, as has been argued.[3] As Ross has commented, Russell was a man of unusual talents and what he says deserves consideration. Certainly the Crowland Chronicler claims to have been as truthful and unbiased as possible, and he was obviously an eye-witness to some of the events he described, such as the scene at Christmas 1484, and in a position to find out about other events. He undoubtedly saw Richard in a bad light, as a dishonest dissembler. Like many (perhaps all) chroniclers of this period, he described events in the light of his own opinions.[4]

(c) Next there is a letter written by the Spaniard Diego de Valera to his monarchs Isabella and Ferdinand of Spain. It was probably based on information derived from Castilian merchants who had recently been in Bristol, and quotes accounts from Juan de Salazar, a captain in the employ of the Emperor Maximilian, who may have been present in

England to help Richard at his master's command. This report is very valuable but rather confused. Salazar had been in England at various times in Richard's reign and it seems very likely that he was with Richard during the last stages of the battle.

(d) In about 1490 the Burgundian Philippe de Commynes wrote the part of his *Memoires* dealing with the reign of Richard III and with the mounting of Tudor's expedition and the events surrounding it. He was at that time in the service of Charles VIII of France and would have had good sources who could inform him of events at this juncture.

(e) The next source to be considered, also written very shortly after the battle, is the Chronicle by the Burgundian Jean Molinet, who died in 1507. He probably wrote his work after 1504. He was historiographer to the court of Burgundy, and his work has some independent value. He was obviously in a position to know what was happening in France and to hear the stories told by the French troops who had been at Bosworth, although interestingly he claims that a Welshman, not a Frenchman, killed Richard.

(f) John Rous wrote his *History of the Kings of England* probably before 1490. A chantry priest in Warwick, he also wrote other works praising his patrons, the Earls of Warwick. His *History* is not very full, and nor is it particularly accurate, except in his account of the royal visit to Warwick. It is very anti-Richard III, in contrast to the fulsome tribute to Richard that occurs in a work Rous finished while Richard was still on the throne. Rous clearly biased his writings in favour of whoever was in power at the time.

(g) The Frenchman Bernard Andre was court poet to Henry VII and tutor to his son. He was thus in a position to talk to eye-witnesses of events, as he himself claimed. He also left gaps where he lacked information, so to some extent he was a conscientious historian (although not conscientious enough to go back later and fill in the gaps). His comment about Richard's burial may thus be factual and not a comment made up after the event to make Henry look like a better person. Even if the reported statement by Henry is accurate, though, it is unfortunately not what actually happened to Richard's body.

(h)   Three extant ballads, entitled 'The Rose of England', 'The Ballad of Bosworth Field' and 'The Song of Lady Bessy', are part of a group of ballads, all written in the Stanley interest, perhaps not long after the battle and probably in the north-west, in Lancashire or Cheshire, as shown by the language and the bias towards that area. The copies that we have now date from the seventeenth century, except for a late sixteenth-century prose paraphrase of 'Bosworth Field'. These ballads would have been transmitted, orally, for many years after the battle. The prose version is sufficiently similar to the poetic version to show that transmission was reasonably accurate, and so perhaps the ballads as we have them are not too far from the original versions. This is important because one of them, the Ballad of Bosworth Field, can be shown to contain checkable facts or details that were or may have been true. For example, it contains a list of Richard's northern supporters, who either we know were there or would have been expected to be there. The list of casualties on Richard's side is likewise almost entirely accurate, and the statement that Sir John Savage commanded a wing of Tudor's army is also true.[5] There is good reason to suppose that the original ballad was written before 1495, well within living memory of the events described, since Sir William Stanley (who was executed for treason in 1495) is described in laudatory terms and his decisive intervention at the end of the battle of Bosworth is also described, which would not have been the case if the ballad had been composed after his death. Similar laudatory references to Sir William appear in the Song of Lady Bessy too, although a verse at the end does admit that Sir William later 'came under a cloud'. Both the Song of Lady Bessy and the Rose of England are more concerned with Lady Elizabeth's plans and plots to marry Henry Tudor than they are with historical events, but there are some nuggets of information in both that can be corroborated by other sources and that must have come from a knowledgeable source. Thus the Rose of England says that Tudor made a flank attack, which only the Burgundian Molinet also says. The author of the ballad is unlikely to have had access to Molinet's work, which only existed in manuscript until 1828.[6] A few of the verses in the Ballad of Bosworth Field also appear in the Song of Lady Bessy, perhaps indicating that they originated from the same source.

(i)   Other sources have been used in this book for the general history of the period, starting with *The Usurpation of Richard III* by Dominic Mancini, an eye-witness to events in England from the summer of 1482 until he left in July 1483. It thus does not cover the later events of Richard's reign but is very valuable for the events that Mancini witnessed. He was a humanist and was sent to England, probably to report on English affairs, by Angelo Cato, Archbishop of Vienne. Mancini probably did not speak English, or at least not very well, and so was mostly reliant for his information on the Italians in England and of course from those educated men who spoke Latin. His work is a detailed and sober account of the events as he saw them. He undoubtedly got his information from central figures at court. He was recalled to France in July 1483 and his report to Cato was completed by December 1483.[7]

Other sources include the London Chronicles, in various versions. These chronicles are centred on London of course, reporting on events as seen or heard about in the capital. They thus have value for events in London but less reliance can be placed on them for events happening elsewhere. Their principal value lies in the fact that they were compiled soon after the events they describe, so they show what was generally believed by London citizens at the time. The ones used for this book are the *Great Chronicle of London* and the chronicles of Robert Fabyan (who also probably wrote the *Great Chronicle of London*). The *History of King Richard III* by Thomas More, edited by Richard Sylvester (1963), has not been used for events in the early years of Richard's reign. His work may or may not embody information obtained from eye-witnesses to events, or from Cardinal John Morton when More was in Morton's household, but much of what he said has been strongly disputed and he undoubtedly embroidered facts. It seemed safer not to use it.

Appendix 2

Commissions of Array

Commissions of array are frequently mentioned in the text, and it seems useful to print a sample of the documents involved. Issuing a commission was a complicated bureaucratic process, and in general a commission had to be sent to all of the counties involved, although it was not uncommon to send commissions just to a restricted area to raise men for a less widespread emergency. Records were kept of each kind of document needed and of everyone to whom they needed to be sent, and a large pool of messengers was maintained to take them. These men would be ordered to deliver the commissions to several people in the same area, as were the messengers who delivered the requests for loans described above. The commission quoted below was addressed to the Gloucester Commissioners and was entered into the Privy Seal Register (now known as Harleian Ms. 433) as an example to be followed for the other areas. The formal commission is preceded in the register by what can be described as general notes for the guidance of the commissioners – they should see that the men were ready, that they were 'no rascals', that money raised for the purposes of this and other commissions was still available and had not been (or would not be) spirited away and finally that they carry out their duties 'at their peril' of the king's severe displeasure.[1]

As seen in the commission itself, immediate action was expected: the men had to be mustered without delay and if necessary kept under arms. The commissioners had to ensure that the men were all suitably clothed and equipped, and to organise them into suitable units. All men were expected to serve but the burden of actually doing so might be expected to fall on the poorer men who could not find a way of getting someone else to serve in their place.[2] The retainers of each lord were expected to be in a state of readiness too, and the two groups, of pressed men and retainers, inevitably overlapped to some extent. The commissioners were usually deliberately chosen as men of influence in the area who could bring their own retinues as well as those responding to the commission. The system worked reasonably well but both sets of men being summoned (retainers and arrayed men) could sometimes be raised by a lord for his own purposes and turned against the king, as seen in the Bosworth campaign where the Stanley forces were turned against Richard. Towns were expected to raise men too, as seen in the case of York.

Commission for the county of Gloucester

Richard by the grace of God King of England and France and lord of Ireland to his very dear kinsman William, Earl of Nottingham, and his loved and faithful Richard Beauchamp of Beauchamp knight, John Beauchamp knight, Thomas Cowkesey knight, Alexander Baynham knight, Thomas Lymeryk, John Huddelstone, Gilbert de Brigys, John Twynyhoo, Nicholas Spycer, Thomas Whitingtone, John Grenehille, Bayneham, Thomas Brige, Thomas Porter, and William Trye and our Sheriff of Gloucester, greeting. Know that for the safety and defence of our kingdom of England against the malice of rebels and our foreign enemies who intend to attack various parts of our said kingdom near the coast, we have appointed you jointly and separately to array and inspect all and singular men-at-arms and all other defensible men, both light horsemen and archers, dwelling within the said county, and when they have been arrayed and inspected in such array, to cause them to be set and put in thousands, hundreds and scores or otherwise as may be convenient and necessary, and lead them or cause them to be led to our presence with all possible speed to attack and expel the aforesaid rebels and enemies from time to time as the need arises from imminent peril. Also to hold and superintend diligently the muster or review of the same men-at-arms, light horsemen and archers from time to time as need shall arise. And we enjoin and command you and each one of you as strictly as we may that on the sight of these presents you will at once cause to be armed and arrayed and to come before you all and singular the defensible and able-bodied men of the said county and array and arm them according to their grades and ranks and when they have been thus arrayed and armed, to keep them in such array. Moreover we give firm command to all and singular our liegemen and subjects of the aforesaid county by tenor of these presents that they shall be in all things submissive, attentive and diligently obedient to you and any of you, in the execution of these presents. In witness whereof we have caused these our letters patent to be made. Witness myself at Westminster the 8th day of December in the second year of our reign.

By the king himself.

Yve

This draft commission is signed by Richard Yve, a clerk of the crown in chancery, who wrote out the document.

Instructions given by the king's grace to the Commissioners appointed in every shire of this his Realm

First that they on the kings behalf thank the people for their true and loving dispositions showed to his highness the last year for the surety and defence of his most royal person and of this his Realm against his rebels and traitors exhorting them so to continue

Item that the said Commissioners incontinent after the Receipt of their commissions diligently enquire of all bailiffs Constables and other Officers of towns, townships, villages and hundreds within the precinct of their Commission the number of persons sufficiently horsed harnessed and arrayed as by every of them severally were granted to do the kings grace service before the old Commissioners when soever his highness should command them for certain days in their said grants expressed for the resisting and subduing of his enemies rebels and traitors and of the same persons and their array to take a good view and see that they be able men and well horsed and harnessed and no rascal and to endeavour them to increase the number by their wisdoms and policies if they can

Item that they also diligently enquire if all such money for the wages of the said persons as in every place hath been gathered and levied and to whose hands and keeping the same was delivered and whether it so resteth or not and thereupon to order and see that the same money be always ready in the Constable or bailiffs hands or other by their discretions delivered to the said persons without any manner delay when they shall be commanded to do the king service and in likewise to order and see in every place where no such money have been gathered and levied that it forthwith be levied and delivered to the hands of the constable bailiffs or other there to remain and surely to be kept for the wages of the persons so by them granted to do his grace service

Item in case that any part of the same money heretofore levied be by any person taken out of the keeping of any of the said Constables bailiffs or other against their wills or otherwise that then the said Commissioners not only see the same restored to the said Constables but also the so taker be committed to ward and punished after their discretions

Item that the said Commissioners at the view of the said persons give them strait commandments to attend upon such Captains as the kings grace shall appoint them to attend upon and on none other. As they will avoid the kings high displeasure at their utmost perils

Item that the said Commissioners on the kings behalf give straightly in commandment to all knights squires gentlemen and other being able men of their bodies to do the kings grace service to prepare and ready them self in their persons so to do when they shall be thereunto warned and commanded without any excuse. As they will avoid the kings high displeasure at their perils

Item that the said Commissioners in all goodly haste certify by writing to the kings grace their ordering of the premises in every behalf with the names of the persons so by them seen and viewed

Item to show to all lords noblemen captains and other that the kings noble pleasure and commandment is that they truly and honourably all manner quarrels grudges rancour and unkindness laid apart attend and execute the kings commandment and every each be loving and assisting to other in the kings quarrels and cause showing them plainly that whosoever attempt or presume the contrary the kings grace will so punish them that all other shall take example by them etc.

Appendix 3

The Act of Attainder against Richard and his Supporters

The Act of Attainder was the parliamentary means by which late fifteenth-century and later Kings of England punished defeated opponents, bypassing a proper judicial trial. It was in effect a punishment for treason. The effect of the act was to extinguish all rights of the person attainted, so that they could neither hold titles nor transmit them, as their 'blood was corrupted'. Richard's supporters at Bosworth were, of course, supporting their lawful king, and so could clearly not have committed treason. The way by which Henry got over this technicality was by back-dating his reign to the day before the battle, and thus he was able to argue that they had been in arms against the lawful king. This, of course, was treason. However, Henry's actions in this matter raised fears and doubts even among his staunchest supporters, and he had to force it through against resistance. It is difficult to see how else Henry could have got round the problem – Richard had undoubtedly been the only lawful king on the battlefield – but it obviously left a nasty taste in the mouths of his contemporaries. In all, 28 people were attainted but by 1495 as many as 20 of the attainders had been reversed, with more reversed by the end of Henry's reign. It is thus true, as the chroniclers say, that Henry showed clemency to the leading Yorkist peers and gentry. He was really in no position to do otherwise, although his clemency in reversing attainders was distinctly meaner than previous kings, in that he nearly always imposed financial penalties on the reversal and usually allowed those courtiers who had been granted the attainted estates to retain them.[1] It is interesting to look in more detail at the statistics concerning attainders. Henry VII attainted 138 men for treason in his reign and reversed 52 of them. As Professor Chrimes points out, this compares unfavourably with the precedents of previous reigns: Henry VI attainted 26 men, and later reversed all of them; Edward IV attainted 140 men and reversed 86; and Richard III attainted 100, 99 of which were reversed under Henry VII.[2]

An Act of Conviction and Attainder[3]

Be it also remembered that a bill, containing the terms of a certain act of conviction and attainder of various people, with a schedule attached to it, was presented before the lord king in the present Parliament, in the tenor that follows:

Every king, prince and liege lord is bound, in proportion to the loftiness of his estate and pre-eminence, to advance and make available impartial justice. For as much as every king, prince and liege lord, the more higher that he be in estate and pre-eminence, the more singularly he is bound to the advancement and proffering of that indifferent virtue justice, promoting and rewarding virtue, and by oppressing and punishing vice; wherefore our sovereign lord, calling unto his blessed remembrance this high and great charge adjoined to his royal majesty and estate, not oblivious nor putting out of his godly mind the unnatural, mischievous and great perjuries, treasons, homicides and murders, in shedding of infants blood, with many other wrongs, odious offences and abominations against God and man, and in especial our said sovereign lord, committed and done by Richard late Duke of Gloucester, calling and naming himself, by usurpation, King Richard the iij[d] the which, with John late Duke of Norfolk, Thomas Earl of Surrey, Francis Lovell knight, Viscount Lovell, Walter Devereux knight, late Lord Ferrers, John Lord Zouch, Robert Harington, Richard Charleton, Richard Ratcliff, William Berkeley of Uley, Robert Brackenbury, Thomas Pilkington, Robert Middleton, James Harington, knights, Walter Hopton, William Catesby, Roger Wake, William Sapcote, Humphrey Stafford, William Clerke of Wenlok, Geoffrey St German, Richard Watkyns, herald of arms, Richard Revyll of Derbyshire, Thomas Pulter of the county of Kent the younger, John Walsh otherwise called Hastings, John Kendall, late secretary to the said Richard late Duke, John Buk, Andrew Ratt and William Brampton of Burford, the xxi day of August, the first year of the reign of our said sovereign lord, assembled to them at Leicester in the county of Leicester a great host, traitorously intending, imagining and conspiring the destruction of the king's royal person, our sovereign liege lord. And they, with the same host, with banners spread, mightily armed and defended with all manner armours, as guns, bows, arrows, spears, glaives, axes and all other manner of artilleries apt or needful to give and advance mighty battle against our said sovereign lord, kept together from the said xxi day to the xxij day of the said month then next following, and they led to a field within the said shire of Leicester, there by great and continued deliberation, traitorously levied war against our said sovereign lord, and his true subjects there being in his service and assistance under a banner of our said sovereign lord, to the subversion of this realm, and common weal of the same.

Wherefore, by the advice and assent of the lords Spiritual and Temporal and of the commons in this present Parliament assembled, and by authority of the same, be it enacted, established and ordained, deemed and declared that the said Richard late Duke of Gloucester, otherwise called King Richard the third, John late Duke of Norfolk, Thomas Earl of Surrey, Francis Lovell knight, Viscount Lovell, Walter Devereux knight, late Lord Ferrers, John Lord Zouch, Robert Harington, Richard Charleton, Richard Ratcliff, William Berkeley of Uley, Robert Brackenbury, Thomas Pilkington, Robert Middleton, James Harington, Walter Hopton, William Catesby, Roger Wake, William Sapcote of the county of Huntingdon, Humphrey Stafford, William Clerke of Wenlok, Geoffrey St German, Richard Watkyns, herald of arms, Richard Revyll of Derbyshire, Thomas Pulter of the county of Kent, John Walsh otherwise called Hastings, John Kendall, late secretary of the said Richard late Duke, John Buk, Andrew Ratt and William Brampton stand and be convicted and attainted of high treason, and disabled and forejudged of all manner of honour, estate, dignity and pre-eminence, and the names of the same, and forfeit to our said sovereign lord and to his heirs all castles, manors, lordships, hundreds, franchises, liberties, privileges, advowsons, nominations, presentations, lands, tenements, rents, services, reversions, portions, annuities, pensions, rights, hereditaments, goods, cattle and debts, whereof they or any other to their use or to the use of any of them, were seised or possessed the said xxi day of August, or any time after, within the realm of England, Ireland, Wales or Calais, or in the marches thereof, in fee simple, fee tail or term of life or lives.

Le roi le veult en toutz pointz.

Appendix 4

Legends

Many legends have grown up around the battle of Bosworth, ranging from the story that Henry Tudor stayed at the Three Tuns in Atherstone to the story that at the Reformation Richard III's bones were thrown into the river Soar and that his coffin was used as a horse trough at the Blue Boar inn, where he traditionally stayed before the battle. It was called the White Boar then, after Richard's badge. The blue boar was the badge of the Earl of Oxford, and thus a safer choice after the battle. It is certainly possible that Richard's bones were thrown in the Soar, although we have no evidence that his remains were exhumed at all, and the other stories are also unlikely to be true: stone coffins were not used in the fifteenth century, and an inn is an unlikely place for a fifteenth-century leader to stay if better accommodation was available – Merevale Abbey in Tudor's case and Leicester castle in Richard III's. There are two traditions connected to the battle that may be true, in some form at least, and these are discussed below, as is a new tradition about the so-called wedding medallion of Henry VII and Elizabeth.

(a) The death of Richard III. There is one theme which occurs in all of the sources, from the earliest to the latest, and this is that Richard III died bravely. Since the overwhelming majority of the sources are overtly hostile to Richard, it seems probable that the manner of his death made a great and favourable impression, for in the fifteenth century a noble death was much admired. It is interesting to list these in chronological order, to show the similarities. Usually, when dramatic stories are repeated they tend to become more and more elaborate, but these do not.

1. The first source is the Castilian Report, written very shortly after the battle, on 1 March 1486. When it became apparent that Richard was losing the battle, Salazar is quoted as saying to the king:

> 'Sire, seek safety. You cannot hope to win this battle for your followers have openly betrayed you.' But the king answered, 'Salazar, God forbid that I yield one foot. This day I will die as king or have the victory.'

Richard then went on to fight and be killed.[1]

2. The next source is John Rous, the chantry priest in Warwick. Despite the bias already described, his account of the death of Richard is similar to Salazar's and the later ones. After describing the circumstances of Richard's death he says:

> For all that let me say the truth to his credit; that he bore himself like a noble soldier and despite his little body and feeble strength, honourably defended himself to his last breath, shouting again and again that he was betrayed and crying Treason, Treason, Treason.[2]

Rous is the only chronicler to mention the cry of treason, but since Warwick is not far from the battlefield he could perhaps have heard it from an eye-witness, although this must have been someone very close to the action, given the din and chaos of battle.

3. The third source is the Crowland Chronicler, who also did not have a favourable opinion of Richard, although he undoubtedly served him, perhaps in a very senior position. Again this makes his comment about the manner of Richard's death worthy of notice:[3]

> As for King Richard he received many mortal wounds and, like a spirited and most courageous prince, fell in battle on the field and not in flight.

4. Molinet, the Burgundian chronicler, writing in the early years of the sixteenth century, may have heard of events from the French soldiers at Bosworth. He says:[4]

> The king bore himself valiantly, according to his destiny and wore the crown on his head but when he saw the disaster and found himself alone on the field he thought to run after the others.

5. The next source to mention the manner of Richard's death is Polydore Vergil. As we have seen above (Appendix 1), Vergil seems to have been a reasonably accurate historian, who claimed to tell the truth. As far as Richard is concerned, his bias caused him to attribute evil or sinister motives for the king's actions, but not to invent the actions. Vergil's description of the death of Richard is not dissimilar to Salazar's reported words, but at greater length:[5]

> The report is that King Richard might have sought to save himself by flight, for they who were about him seeing the soldiers even from the first stroke to lift up their weapons faintly and feebly and some of them to depart the field privily, suspected treason and exhorted him to fly and when his cause manifestly began to fail they brought him swift horses but he, who was not ignorant that the people hated him, out of hope to have better success later, is said, such was his great fierceness and force of mind, to have answered that very day he would make an end either of war or life. Wherefore knowing certainly that that day would either yield him a peaceable and quiet realm from henceforth or else perpetually take it away forever he came to the field with the crown upon his head, that he might thereby make a beginning or an end of his reign.

At the end, more succinctly, Vergil writes:

his courage also high and fierce which failed him not in the very death, which, when his men forsook him, he yielded only to the sword rather than by foul flight to prolong his life.

6. Keeping to our chronological order, the next sources to describe Richard's death are Edward Hall and Raphael Holinshed, but these two chroniclers basically used Vergil's text, only adding a few details occasionally, but not about the king's death.

7. The last sources independently giving any information about the way Richard died are the ballads, as described in Appendix 1: the Rose of England, the Song of the Lady Bessy and the Ballad of Bosworth Field. The accounts of Richard's death are similar in the last two, but the Rose of England barely mentions it. The Ballad of Bosworth Field has:

> Then to King Richard there came a knight
> And said, 'I hold it time for to flee
> For yonder Stanleys they be so wight
> Against them no man may dree
> Here is thy horse at thy hand ready
> Another day may thy worship win
> And for to reign with royalty
> To wear the crown and be our king.'
> He said, 'Give me my battleaxe in my hand
> Set the crown of England on my head so high
> For by him that shaped both sea and land
> King of England this day I will die
> One foot will I never flee
> Whilst the breath is my breast within.'
> As he said, so did it be
> If he lost his life if he were king.[6]

(b) The second tradition to be discussed is 'the crown in the thornbush'. There is a persistent later story that the crown with which Lord

Stanley crowned Henry VII on the battlefield was found in a thornbush (i.e., a hawthorn bush). It is Polydore Vergil who first describes a battlefield coronation of the new king, saying 'which when Thomas Stanley did see, he set anon King Richard's crown which was found among the spoil on the field upon his [Henry's] head'.[7] This is copied by Hall. The earliest reference to the crown being found under (or in) a thornbush comes possibly early in the seventeenth century in a manuscript of Sir William Segar, Garter King of Arms. However, there is no doubt that Henry VII did use a badge of a crown and thornbush, and there is a roof boss in the choir of Winchester Cathedral of a bush with a crown on it. This dates from between 1503 and 1509, and there are many similar badges in the Henry VII chapel in Westminster Abbey. The badge of a hawthorn bush, leaves or flowers was used well before Henry VII, mostly by the house of Lancaster, and was so used afterwards by the Tudors.[8] It seems very likely that Henry VII decided to add the crown to the existing badge of the hawthorn bush; we do not know why, but it is possible that it was because his new crown was indeed found under a thornbush.

The actual crown that was used in the battlefield ceremony has usually been assumed to be a coronet which fitted around Richard's helmet. Such crowns are known from manuscript illustrations of battles, and we know that Henry V wore one at Agincourt because it is said to have been knocked off his helmet during the battle.[9]

However, it has been argued recently that Richard carried out a formal crown-wearing ceremony before the battle, a solemn ritual re-enacting his coronation and designed to inspire his army.[10] It is said that the crown used for this ceremony was the crown of St Edward, a sacred relic used at the coronation. This was sometimes known as the 'most precious crown' and the Crowland Chronicle says that Henry was crowned on the battlefield 'with the priceless [or most precious] crown which King Richard had previously worn'.[11] The allusion to 'previously worn' can most simply be understood as worn before or during the battle, i.e., around his helmet. It seems most unlikely that St Edward's crown, sometimes called 'the most excellent crown' in inventories, which was a sacred relic, would be taken from the monks at Westminster Abbey (the custodians of the coronation regalia) and then returned to the abbey after use. St Edward's crown was not the personal property of the king: for that, he had an 'Imperial' crown, which he wore after the coronation ceremony and on other occasions. It is possible that Richard took his own Imperial crown to the battlefield. That the crown on the battlefield was valuable in a monetary sense is stated by the Castilian Report, which says that Richard wore 'the crown royal' worth 120,000 crowns. The unreliable Scottish Pittscottie's Chronicle says that the crown was stolen briefly from Richard's tent by a Scotsman called Macgregor, presumably because it was valuable. However, it does seem unnecessary to interpret the words used in the Crowland Chronicle into anything more than that Richard had a very valuable crown with him. He may have undertaken a crown–wearing ceremony; if he did take his crown, it must have been for some purpose, but what this was we do not know. None of the sources describes anything resembling a formal crown–wearing ceremony.

(c) The wedding medallion of Henry VII and Elizabeth of York. The medallion illustrated opposite has appeared several times in the past 35 years in different books and articles, where it is described as a gold medallion commemorating the marriage of King Henry VII and Elizabeth of York. It is unclear when this identification was first used, but there is no doubt at all that the medallion does not commemorate this wedding. It was mentioned, only to be discounted, in a book of 1885.[12] It was undoubtedly struck to commemorate a wedding, as the obverse inscription reads *Iungimus optatas sub amico foedere dextras* ('We join in a loving union the right hands we have longed for') and on the reverse it reads *Sicut sol oriens dei sic mulier bona domus eius ornamentum* ('As is God's rising sun so also is a good woman an ornament of her house'). The obverse depicts a couple holding hands, the man crowned with a chaplet of roses, and the reverse bears the inscription *Uxor casta est rosa suavis* ('A chaste wife is a sweet rose') within a chaplet of roses. The word for chastity is made to stand out by means of more elaborate lettering. It seems probable that the misidentification came about because of the rose symbolism, as the marriage of Henry and Elizabeth was said to represent the union of the 'roses' of York and Lancaster. However, if the medallion had been struck to commemorate this marriage, it would have been made much more clear in the inscriptions, and certainly the political symbolism would have been made very obvious. In addition, the fact that the man is wearing a wreath while the bride is wearing a crown is not what Henry VII would have wanted. He was a crowned king by the time of the marriage, which had been delayed until after his coronation, and he made it quite clear that his claim to the throne did not depend on Elizabeth. In fact the medallion is one of a series struck in Prague in the late sixteenth century, and medals of English workmanship did not appear until the later sixteenth century. The couple on the medallion have not been identified, if indeed they represent a particular couple and are not merely symbolic of marriage in general.

The late sixteenth-century wedding medallion. (*Geoffrey Wheeler*)

Appendix 5

A Yorkist Soldier at Bosworth

It will have been seen above that we know quite a lot about the leaders on both sides at the battle but we know very little indeed about the common soldiers who made up the vast bulk of the armies. These men were mostly not wealthy, and many of them were poor and left very little record of their existence. Occasionally there are surviving lists of names of the men who were recruited for a particular campaign, for example the men listed in the accounts of John Howard, Duke of Norfolk, in 1484 as promised to the king (see above, pp. 77–8), but this is a rare survival in the late fifteenth century. Commanders must have had lists of their men in order to pay them; there would have been lists of the men recruited by York for the Bosworth campaign, for example, since they were paid, but no list survives. However, there has recently come to light a record of the name of one common soldier who undoubtedly fought at Bosworth, probably in the retinue of the Earl of Surrey.[1]

This record is in the form of the will made by one Thomas Longe, who lived in Ashwellthorpe in Norfolk. Ashwellthorpe was one of the manors held by the Earl of Surrey through his wife Elizabeth Tilney, and thus it seems almost certain that Longe was one of the men recruited by Surrey. We know that Longe fought at Bosworth because his will, a nuncupative will, made verbally before witnesses, states that he made his will on 16 August 1485, 'the said day and time going forth unto the king's host at Nottingham to battle'. He left all his goods movable and immovable, together with any cattle he owned at his death, to his wife Joan and to one William Herward. These two were also made his executors. His witnesses were named as Richard and William Partryk (or Partridge), who may have been fellow soldiers. If so, they survived Bosworth since they appear as jurors in a case in Ashwellthorpe in 1505. We do not know where Longe was when the will was made, although it may have been at Bury St Edmunds, where John Howard ordered his troops to muster by the 16th, as seen above (p. 67). Surrey his son may have ordered the same mustering place.

Thomas Longe appears only once more in the documentary records, as an executor in a will made in February 1483, and the family does not appear in the few local records. He was obviously not a very poor man, given that he had cattle as well as other goods to bequeath, but it seems unlikely that he was a man of great substance. Since he was preparing to be a soldier, he was presumably in good health and in the prime of life. He would have seen no reason previously to make his will in a more orthodox way by going to a scribe to have it written, and so made it this way on his journey to join the king's army. It was not uncommon for soldiers to make a nuncupative will in front of witnesses before going into battle and it was perfectly legal. It still is for soldiers on active service.

We do not know if Longe survived the battle but his will was proved on 14 January 1486, when probate was granted to his widow. It is probable that he was either killed at Bosworth or, more likely, given the length of time between the battle and proving the will, was wounded and only lived a short while after. We will never know what his experiences were in the battle, nor what part he played – perhaps he was an archer – but whatever he did, and whatever happened, we now know the name of one of the common soldiers who fought for their king on 22 August 1485.

Appendix 6

Epilogue

What happened after the battle of Bosworth is described at the end of chapter 6. Richard's body was taken to Leicester and, after exposure in a church to prove that he was undoubtedly dead, he was buried in the Greyfriars Priory. A tomb was afterwards erected by Henry VII. We know very little about the tomb, not even whether it was a table tomb or a simple slab. Its location was known roughly and after the Reformation, when the site of the Greyfriars became a garden, a column was placed on the site of the tomb. This column had long disappeared and the site had become a car park when, in mid-summer 2012, after a survey of the site, excavations were started by Leicester University Archaeological Department.[1]

In a very short time a grave was found containing a single skeleton. It was in an area identified by the archaeologists as the choir of the Franciscan church, which was where a contemporary historian said Richard was buried.[2] The bones were found in an apparently hastily dug grave with sloping sides and a concave base. It was too small for the body, which was apparently laid in the grave feet first; since the grave was too short, this meant that the top of the body had to be contorted to get it in, with the skull twisted to one side. The arms were crossed over the pelvis, somewhat unusually for a Leicester burial.[3] This burial posture could have been caused by the body having been carried to Leicester over the back of a horse with the hands tied to help balance the body. There was no evidence for a coffin or a shroud. The person was male and had apparently died violently: there were two wounds in the skull, either of which could have killed the man. The bones were thus those of someone who had died in battle. The feet and one leg bone were missing, apparently removed long after death, perhaps in Victorian times when the area was redeveloped. From the evidence it seemed very likely that the body of Richard III had been found.

Further examination showed that the identification of the bones as those of Richard III was almost certain. The man had scoliosis (that is, a spine twisted into an S-shaped curve). This would probably have made the man's right shoulder higher than his left, but it would not have caused him to have a hunchback, as later Tudor chroniclers said. Richard III was said by early chroniclers to have one shoulder higher than the other. The scoliosis is likely to have developed at the onset of puberty and would probably have caused a certain amount of pain, although if it did it was obviously not enough to prevent him taking part in martial exercises. The bones showed that Richard did not have a withered arm, as the later Tudor chroniclers claimed. Richard's height in life would naturally have been about 5ft 8in (1.72m), tall for the time, although the scoliosis would have reduced this by several inches. The bones show that Richard was of an unusually slender build for a man. This fits with the description of him by John Rous as 'small of body and feeble of limb'.[4] The age at death was estimated as between 30 and 33 years old, and radiocarbon dating showed that this individual died in the second half of the fifteenth century or early sixteenth century. Both of these results are consistent with the bones being those of Richard III, who died aged 33 in 1485. Consistent with the high status of Richard III, the bones showed evidence of a high-protein diet, including much seafood, and the teeth showed signs of dental caries, as might be expected from a diet rich in sugars and carbohydrates, again consistent with high status.[5] Identification was finally confirmed by mitochondrial DNA extracted from the teeth, which matched that extracted from two maternal-line descendants of his sisters. Mitochondrial DNA is transmitted from mother to child, and there is usually no change between generations.[6]

Having proved, with little room for doubt, that the bones were those of Richard III, the bones were examined in an effort to obtain information on how he died. As seen in chapter 6, Richard III was killed after a desperate cavalry charge designed to put an end to the battle at a stroke. This charge could not have been undertaken on the spur of the moment, however, as Vergil implies. A cavalry charge requires preparation both on the part of the horses and the men, and Richard must have known beforehand that he might do this and warned his men. It nearly worked, but at some point Richard must have been unhorsed. He would almost certainly not have been knocked unconscious by his fall, and his armour would have protected him from injury; as a trained fighter, he would have sprung to his feet again and continued the fight. Of course it is possible that he was immediately restrained by his opponents and if, as some chroniclers say, he fell in boggy ground this might slow down his reactions.[7]

There was evidence of damage to various parts of the body but two severe wounds, one perhaps caused by a halberd-like staff weapon and one perhaps by a sword, were found on the skull, either of which could have killed him.[8] Both were delivered from behind and went through from the base of the skull into the brain.[9] There was also a hole in the top of the skull that was perhaps caused by a dagger, but this would not have killed him. These blows could not have been delivered while Richard wore his helmet, as he would have done in his final charge. The injuries must have been inflicted after he was unhorsed and his helmet had been removed. It could not have fallen off when he was unhorsed, as it was designed not to fall off whatever type of helmet he was wearing. In fact, he almost certainly wore some type of sallet, the usual English helmet. It would have had to be removed by either undoing or cutting the chinstrap, or perhaps simply wrenching it forcibly away. Richard is unlikely to have taken it off himself, so it was most likely removed by his enemies while he was restrained or unconscious. The other minor wounds on the body must have been inflicted after death when the body had been stripped of armour, and were probably inflicted as humiliation wounds.

The surviving contemporary accounts tell us little about how Richard died, although Molinet (see chapter 6) said that Richard was killed by a Welsh halberdier, and we now have evidence that he was perhaps killed by a halberd or halberd-like weapon. Recently it has been suggested that he was killed by a Welshman (sometimes called an Englishman) called William Gardiner. There is no evidence at all for the existence of such a man. Due to the renewed likelihood that Richard was killed by a blow from a halberd, the story that he was killed by Rhys ap Thomas has been revived (see p. 103). The Welsh poet Guto'r Glynn said of Rhys that 'he killed the boar, he shaved his head' – and this has now been interpreted literally rather than metaphorically to indicate that Rhys shaved Richard's skull with his weapon.[10]

These results show at last how Richard III died, and the bones show us what kind of man he was physically. All of this is valuable information and helps us to understand him as a man. Unfortunately, of course, they tell us nothing about his thoughts and the reasons behind his actions.

Notes and References

Abbreviations

The following abbreviations are used in the Notes. Full citations of the works briefly described below will be found in the Bibliography. Works cited only by the author's name in the notes are not given below but will be found in the Bibliography under that author.

BBF	The Ballad of Bosworth Field
Castilian Report	Goodman and McKay, 'A Castilian Report on English Affairs'
CC	*Crowland Chronicle Continuations, 1459–1486*
CChR	*Calendar of Charter Rolls*, vol. 6
CCR	*Calendar of Close Rolls, 1476–1485*
Coronation	Anne F. Sutton and P.W. Hammond, *The Coronation of Richard III: the Extant Documents*
CPR	*Calendar of Patent Rolls, 1476–1485*
Crown and People	J. Petre, *Richard III: Crown and People*
EHR	*English Historical Review*
Foedera	Thomas Rymer, *Foedera, Conventiones etc.*
Great Chronicle	*The Great Chronicle of London*, ed. A.H. Thomas and I.D. Thornley
Harl. 433	Rosemary Horrox and P.W. Hammond, *British Library Harleian Manuscript 433*
Household Books	*Household Books of John Howard, Duke of Norfolk*
IPM	*Calendar of Inquisitions Post Mortem, Henry VII*
Itinerary	Rhoda Edwards, *The Itinerary of Richard III, 1483–1485*
LB	Ballad: The Most Pleasant Song of the Lady Bessy
Letters and Papers	James Gairdner (ed.), *Letters and Papers Illustrative of the Reigns of Richard III and Henry VII*

PV	Polydore Vergil, *Three Books of Polydore Vergil's English History*
PV (Hay)	Polydore Vergil, *The Anglica Historia of Polydore Vergil*, ed. Denys Hay
Road to Bosworth Field	P.W. Hammond and Anne F. Sutton, *Richard III: the Road to Bosworth Field*
YHB	Lorraine C. Attreed, *York House Books, 1461–1490*

Preface

1. YHB, vol. 1, p. 368; vol. 2, pp. 735–6.
2. Green, p. 589.
3. The origin of the name Redmoor is discussed by Foss, pp. 33–5, and Sandford, p. 38.
4. Thornton, pp. 436–42.
5. Great Chronicle, p. 237; Foss, p. 23.
6. Coote and Thornton, p. 329.

Prologue

1. YHB, vol. 1, p. 282. David Palliser has suggested that the clerk of the council had mistakenly dated his entry 'vij' instead of 'xij', meaning the news arrived on 11 April, a more likely date. Palliser, pp. 51–81; HMC, vol. 18, 11th Report (1887), p. 170, a letter to King's Lynn.
2. Mancini, pp. 70–3; CC, p. 155.
3. CC, p. 155; Mancini, pp. 70, 72–3.
4. YHB, vol. 1, p. 282; vol. 2, p. 712; Victoria County History of Yorkshire: the City of York (1982), p. 65, citing R.R. Reid, *King's Council in the North* (1921).
5. Mancini, pp. 70–1, 115.
6. Rous (Hanham), p. 118.
7. CC, p. 157; Mancini, pp. 76–9.
8. For a discussion of the complicated sequence of events from 29 April to 4 May, see Armstrong in Mancini, pp. 116–17, notes 46–52.
9. Mancini, p. 119, note 59; Harl. 433, vol. 1, p. 3.
10. Mancini, pp. 80–3.
11. Mancini, pp. 82–3; Great Chronicle, p. 230.
12. CC, p. 157.
13. Roskell, pp. 227–8; CC, p. 157.
14. Green, p. 588; Mancini, pp. 84–5.
15. CPR, p. 348.

16. Mancini, pp. 78–81; CC, p. 157; Ross, p. 73.
17. Mancini, p. 91, and note 84.
18. Mancini, pp. 80–1 and p. 119, note 59.
19. Harl. 433, vol. 3, pp. 1, 2; Mancini, pp. 84–7.
20. Harl. 433, vol. 1, p. 7; Household Books, pp. 391, 392.
21. Harl. 433, vol. 1, pp. 9–15, 16–17; Mancini, p. 83.
22. Stonor Letters, vol. 2, p. 161; Harl. 433, vol. 1, pp. 19–20; vol. 3, pp. 11–12; CCR, no. 1035.
23. Stonor Letters, vol. 2, p. 160.
24. Coronation, p. 19, note 53.
25. YHB, vol. 1, pp. 283–4.
26. YHB, vol. 1, pp. 284–6; vol. 2, pp. 713–14.
27. Paston Letters, vol. 3, p. 306.
28. Ross, p. 82.
29. Commynes (transl. Jones), pp. 353, 397, and see discussion in Kendall, pp. 215–19, 476–7 and note 18; Horrox, pp. 112–14.
30. Rous (Hanham), pp. 121–2; Green, p. 588; Mancini, p. 91: CC, p. 159.
31. Mancini, p. 91; CC, p. 159. For a discussion of the execution of Hastings and the possibility of a plot, see Ross, pp. 80–5 and Wood, pp. 155–68.
32. Mancini, p. 89; CC, p. 159; Stonor Letters, vol. 2, p. 161; YHB, vol. 1, p. 284.
33. Coronation, p. 22, notes 77 and 80.
34. Acts of Court of the Mercers Company, p. 155; Stonor Letters, vol. 2, p. 161.
35. Rous (Hanham), p. 119; Mancini, p. 126, note 85; CC, p. 161.
36. Mancini, p. 93; CC, p. 161.
37. Mancini, p. 94.
38. CC, p. 161; *Letters and Papers*, vol. 1, pp. 11–13. For the complicated chronology of events at the end of June, see Coronation, pp. 24–5. The grounds on which Richard claimed the throne have been discussed at considerable length. See for example Ross, pp. 88–93.
39. CChR, vol. 6, p. 258; Foedera, vol. 12, p. 190; Harl. 433, vol. 1, p. 65.
40. Mancini, pp. 99–101, 132, note 104. Armstrong points out that Edward IV overawed London with a force of armed men on the occasion of his coronation.

The New King

1. For the events of 6 July and the subsequent few days see Coronation, pp. 35–46.
2. CPR, pp. 359, 361, 363.
3. Harl. 433, vol. 1, p. 75; vol. 3, pp. 36–8; CPR, p. 403.

4. Rous (Hanham), p. 122; Harl. 433, vol. 3, pp. 23–6; *Letters and Papers*, vol. 1, pp. 23–5, 31–3.
5. Harl. 433, vol. 2, pp. 24–5.
6. Harl. 433, vol. 1, pp. 81–3. Concerning the duchy of Cornwall, it is probable that Richard III regarded himself as the heir to Edward the Black Prince, 1st Duke of Cornwall, thus making his son automatically duke on his own accession. See Complete Peerage, vol. III, pp. 440–1.
7. YHB, vol. 1, p. 287; vol. 2, p. 713; Rous (Hanham), p. 122; Harrison, pp. 111–12.
8. YHB, vol. 1, pp. 288, 290–2; Harrison, pp. 111–12.
9. Coronation, pp. 178–9.
10. YHB, vol. 1, pp. 291–2, 295–6.
11. Harl. 433, vol. 1, pp. 1–2, 81–3; Rous (Hanham), p. 122; PV, p. 190; CC, p. 161; Harrison, p. 112.
12. Harl. 433, vol. 1, pp. 120, 224; vol. 2, pp. 17; YHB, vol. 2, p. 729.
13. YHB, vol. 1, pp. 296, 297; Hairsine, pp. 81–2.
14. CC, p. 163; Ramsay, vol. 2, p. 504.
15. Rolls of Parliament, vol. 6, p. 245.
16. Ross, p. 116; Paston Letters, vol. 2, pp. 442–3.
17. Paston Letters, vol. 3, p. 308; Plumpton Correspondence, pp. 44–5.
18. CPR, p. 370; Gairdner, p. 131.
19. Gairdner, p. 138, quoting Seyer, *Memoirs of Bristol*, vol. 2 (1823); CC, p. 105.
20. CPR, p. 368; Ramsay, vol. 2, p. 506; CC, p. 165; Gairdner, p. 136.
21. PV, p. 202; CC, p. 169; Griffiths and Thomas, p. 102. For a discussion of this complicated episode, see Horrox, pp. 151–60, also Kendall, p. 482, note 13.
22. Arthurson and Kingwell, pp. 102–4.
23. Ross, pp. 118–24 analyses the results of the rebellion.
24. Harl. 433, vol. 2, pp. 66–7; CC, pp. 169, 173.
25. Ross, p. 196; Gairdner, p. 152.
26. Harl. 433, vol. 2, p. 63. See also Kendall, p. 279.
27. Harl. 433, vol. 2, pp. 44, 45, 48–9, 69, 75–7, 90.
28. Rolls of Parliament, vol. 6, pp. 240–2.
29. CC, pp. 170–1. The wording of the oath was probably similar to that taken by leading men, including the Duke of Gloucester, to Prince Edward, son of Edward IV, in 1471, CCR, p. 229.
30. Harl. 433, vol. 3, p. 190.
31. Baldwin, *The Lost Prince* (2007), p. 81; Hampton, pp. 176–83.
32. PV, p. 210.

Preparing for Invasion

1. Harl. 433, vol. 2, pp. 72, 82, 112; CPR, pp. 385, 405, 448; Kendall, p. 293.
2. *Itinerary*, pp. 15–27.
3. Charles Cooper, *Annals of Cambridge*, vol. 1 (8142), pp. 228–9, 230. 'Servants' is here mistranslated as 'minstrels'.
4. CC, pp. 170–1. The misunderstanding over the date may have been due to misreading the *Crowland Chronicle*. There is no evidence to show that Edward died on 31 March, as stated in CP, vol. 5, p. 742 (see vol. 14, p. 341). For the 'Castle of Care', see Kendall, p. 290.
5. Dobson, *Richard III and the Church of York*, pp. 145–6. Dobson discusses the possibility that Richard may have intended to be buried there himself.
6. CC, pp. 172–3; Armstrong, p. 107, note 6.
7. CPR, pp. 397, 399, 400 and 401 for Yorkshire, Westmorland and Cumberland.
8. CC, pp. 172–3.
9. Rous (Hanham), p. 123.
10. Harl. 433, vol. 3, pp. 107–8; CPR, p. 477; *Letters and Papers*, vol. 1, p. 56.
11. *Itinerary*, p. 19.
12. Foedera, vol. 12, pp. 235, 244; *Letters and Papers*, vol. 1, pp. 63–7.
13. Foedera, vol. 12, p. 226; CPR, p. 446.
14. Foedera, vol. 12, p. 229; CPR, p. 446.
15. PV, p. 205; Harl. 433, vol. 2, p. 163; Griffiths and Thomas, p. 111; Ross, pp. 198, 199; Goodman and Mackay, p. 95; Nokes and Wheeler, pp. 4–5.
16. PV, pp. 205–7; Gairdner, pp. 168–9; Chrimes, *Henry VII*, p. 31; Ross, p. 201.
17. Kendall, p. 302 and note 22; Ross, p. 202; Scofield, pp. 244–5; PV, pp. 212–13; Harl. 433, vol. 1, p. 230; vol. 2, p. 188; CPR, p. 526; Foedera, vol. 12, pp. 265–6.
18. Harl. 433, vol. 2, p. 182; vol. 3, pp. 125–6.
19. Harl. 433, vol. 3, pp. 124–5; Ramsay, p. 536; Ross, pp. 208–9.
20. BL Harleian Ms. 787, f2b, printed in full in Hutton, *Bosworth* (1813), pp. 190–1.
21. Hutton, *Bosworth* (1813), pp. 192–3.
22. CPR, p. 520; Holinshed quoted in Gairdner, p. 186.
23. CC, pp. 173, 175. The translation given here is based partly on the Pronay and Cox edition, partly on the older version by Riley (1893) and partly on advice from Lesley Boatwright to whom I am grateful. See comments by Gairdner, pp. 203–5.
24. CC, p. 175.

25. Harl. 433, vol. 3, pp. 128–33; Ramsay, pp. 532–3; CC, pp. 173, 175.
26. CC, 175; Sutton, pp. 16–17.
27. PV, pp. 210–11. The historian John Rous goes so far as to accuse Richard of deliberately poisoning his wife: Rous (Hanham), p. 121.
28. CC, p. 175.
29. CC, pp. 175, 177; PV, p. 212; the king was in the Priory of St John's on 30 March, according to the minutes of the Mercers' Company; Acts of Court, pp. 173–4.
30. Buck, p. 191; John Ashdown-Hill, *Richard III's 'beloved cousyn'* (2009), p. 113 and note 21; Livia Visser-Fuchs, *The Ricardian Bulletin* (Spring 2005), pp. 18–20.
31. YHB, vol. 1, pp. 359–60.
32. See Barrie Williams, 'The Portuguese Connection and the Significance of the Holy Princess', pp. 138–45, 'The Portuguese Marriage Negotiations: a Reply', pp. 235–6.
33. Harl. 433, vol. 1, p. 82.
34. Harl. 433, vol. 3, pp. 124, 139.
35. PV, pp. 210, 214; Griffiths and Thomas, pp. 126–7.
36. CPR, pp. 532, 535.
37. PV, p. 215.
38. Foedera, vol. 12, pp. 255, 260, 261; Griffiths and Thomas, p. 121.
39. Griffiths and Thomas, pp. 129–31; Commynes (trans. Jones), pp. 355, 397; PV, pp. 201, 214, 216; Molinet, vol. 2, p. 406; Conway, pp. 6–7; Antonovics, pp. 176–7; Spont, p. 394. See also the discussion of the size of Tudor's army, below, pp. 75–6.
40. CPR, p. 545; CC, p. 177.
41. Harl. 433, vol. 1, p. 112; vol. 2, pp. 189, 197; PV, p. 213; Ramsay, vol. 2, p. 535.
42. Harl. 433, vol. 2, pp. 228–9.
43. YHB, vol. 1, pp. 366–7.
44. Harl. 433, vol. 2, p. 230 (this copy is incomplete); Paston Letters, vol. 3, pp. 316–20; Griffiths and Thomas, pp. 28, 31.
45. CCR, items 1457, 1458.
46. Condon (1986), p. 9.

The Invasion
1. PV, p. 215; Griffiths and Thomas, p. 115.
2. 'Judge me, O Lord, and defend my cause', psalm 42, Great Chronicle, p. 237. Robert Fabyan adds that he also asked his soldiers to follow him in the name

of the Lord and St George; Griffiths, 'Henry Tudor, the training of a king', p. 207.

3. The other knights dubbed here were David Owen, Edward Poynings, John Fortescue and James Blunt. The latter two had joined Tudor with Oxford when the earl escaped from Hammes castle, Gairdner, p. 363. For the peerage creations and restorations see Complete Peerage under the individual titles.

4. PV, p. 216; Chrimes, 'The Landing Place of Henry of Richmond, 1485', pp. 173–80; Harris, 'The Transmission of the News of the Tudor Landing', pp. 5–12.

5. PV, pp. 216–17; Griffiths and Thomas, pp. 137–9. Tudor's letter is quoted from Griffiths, p. 139.

6. W.T. Williams, pp. 33–41; Griffiths and Thomas, pp. 140–7.

7. PV, pp. 217–18.

8. Griffiths and Thomas, p. 148; Griffiths, article on Rhys ap Thomas in Oxford DNB.

9. Owen and Blakeway, vol. 2, p. 530.

10. Griffiths and Thomas, pp. 149–50; Campbell, vol. 1, p. 156.

11. Campbell, vol. 2, pp. 110–11.

12. PV, p. 218; Griffiths and Thomas, pp. 151–2.

13. BBF, p. 250.

14. PV, pp. 220–1; Hutton, p. 54. Hutton gives reasons why it would be easy to mistake the road to Tamworth and take a fork to Whittington.

15. PV, p. 221; Griffiths and Thomas, p. 154; Campbell, vol. 1, p. 365; D. Williams, p. 90.

16. CC, p. 181; Campbell, vol. 1, pp. 188, 201, 233.

17. BBF, p. 250.

18. Hutton, *Bosworth* (1813), p. 66.

Preparing to Receive the Invader
1. CC, p. 177; *Road to Bosworth Field*, pp. 212–13; Paston Letters, vol. 2, pp. 443–4; YHB, vol. 1, p. 367; Kendall, p. 348.

2. Goodman and Mackay, pp. 136–7.

3. PV, p. 220.

4. Ross, pp. 213–14; YHB, vol. 1, pp. 367–8, vol. 2, p. 735; Goodman and Mackay, p. 222.

5. CC, p. 179.

6. CC, p. 179.

7. Ms. 590 1485, Warrington Public Library; Crown and People, p. 260.

8. Holland, pp. 854, 855–6.

9. CC, p. 179; PV, pp. 219–20; Harl. 433, vol. 3, p. 28.
10. PV, p. 219.
11. Foss, pp. 46–7.
12. Holinshed (1577), vol. 4, p. 1416; Glen Foard, Press Release, Leicester County Council, 28 October 2009.
13. CC, p. 181; D. Williams, p. 89.
14. PV, p. 221; Coventry Leet Book, part 2, p. 531.

Military Matters
1. Molinet, vol. 2, pp. 406–7; PV, p. 216; Griffiths, p. 129; Antonovics, pp. 173, 175–6.
2. Nokes and Wheeler, p. 2; Goodman and McKay, p. 95.
3. Lesley Boatwright, pp. 61–3; Baldwin, pers. comm.; Ross, p. 215.
4. Fiorato et al. This book analyses the equipment brought by the men. Thanks are due to Professor Anne Curry for drawing my attention to the Bridport muster roll at the Bosworth conference, 20 Februry 2010.
5. Household Books, pp. 480–90.
6. Campbell, vol. 1, p. 9; PV, p. 223.
7. Vale, p. 149.
8. LB, pp. 324, 360; BBF, p. 258.
9. Barnard, p. 1; Goodman and Mackay, p. 163.
10. PV, p. 222; Mancini, p. 99.
11. Mancini, p. 99.
12. Dillon, 'How a man shall be armed at his ease when he shall fight on foot', pp. 43 *et seq.*
13. Foard, pp. 26–7; BBF, pp. 253, 254.
14. BBF, p. 253.
15. Foard, map 2, p. 29; Molinet, vol. 2, p. 407.
16. Contamine, pp. 231–2.
17. Flavius Vegetius Renatus, *De Re Militari* ('Concerning Military Matters').
18. Contamine, p. 232.

The Battle
1. Warnicke, 'Lord Morley's statement about Richard III', pp. 173–8 and 'Sir Ralph Bygod: a Loyal Servant to King Richard III', p. 299; Williams, p. 89.
2. CC, p. 181; Kendall, p. 358. Kendall believed that a lack of chaplains is perfectly likely.
3. Ashdown-Hill, 'The Bosworth Crucifix', pp. 83–96.
4. CC, p. 181; Hall, pp. 414–16.

5. Hall, p. 419.
6. Hall, p. 414, is the earliest of these, followed by Holinshed (1587), p. 755. Since the wording is nearly identical, Hall is presumably Holinshed's source here.
7. PV, p. 223; Hutton, *Bosworth* (1813), prose summary of BBF, p. 216.
8. PV, p. 222, 225; Molinet, p. 408.
9. Goodman and Mackay, p. 92.
10. BBF, pp. 251–2. The Song of Lady Bessy has Lord Stanley agreeing to let his rearguard join Tudor under Sir William Stanley, pp. 358–9; PV, p. 222.
11. William Burton, *Description of Leicestershire* (1622), p. 168, cited in D. Williams, p. 93.
12. CC, p. 181.
13. Campbell, vol. 1, p. 188. The others knighted here were Richard Gifford, John Halwey (probably Sir John Halwell, later Sheriff of Devonshire in the first year of Henry VII), John Riseley, John Treury, William Tyler and Thomas Milborn; see Gairdner, p. 364.
14. PV, p. 223.
15. The French league was about 3,200 yards, R.D. Connor, *The Weights and Measures of England* (1987), p. 76; PV, p. 223; Griffiths and Thomas, p. 161.
16. CC, p. 181; Gravett, pp. 60–1. Gravett places the two Stanleys together on the slopes of Dadlington Hill; for further comment on this, see below.
17. CC, p. 181; BBF, pp. 253–5; LB, pp. 359–61; D. Williams, p. 91.
18. PV, p. 223.
19. Molinet, p. 408; the credit for the flank attack is given entirely to the French troops by Molinet. The Rose of England ballad also says that Oxford made a flank attack, p. 194.
20. PV, p. 223.
21. Contamine, p. 232.
22. Grant, pp. 129–30; Goodman, p. 166.
23. LB, p. 361. The badge was an eagle displayed; Foard, p. 25. Several families used such a badge; the most likely here is perhaps the Greys of Ruthyn, Earls of Kent. George Grey, a commissioner of array for Richard, and son and heir of the elderly earl, may have been there with retainers, one of whom lost his badge. BBF, p. 244 says that the earl himself was there.
24. PV, pp. 223, 224.
25. Jones, pp. 193–5. Jones was the first person to draw attention to this letter. The letter writer also claims that Richard charged with 15,000 men, an exaggeration probably designed to show his bravery in helping defeat such a force.
26. PV, p. 224; BBF, p. 252.

27. Harris, 'Tudor Heraldry at Bosworth', p. 130. The Castilian Report says that afterwards it became apparent that Tamorlant had intended to place on the throne not Henry Tudor but the Earl of Warwick, son of the Duke of Clarence, presumably intending to kill both Tudor and Richard; Goodman and McKay, p. 97. This seems unlikely.

28. Quoted from Gairdner, p. 244.

29. For the death of Richard as described in the sources, see below, Appendix 4. PV, p. 224; Nokes and Wheeler, p. 2; Hanham, pp. 55–6; BBF, pp. 256–7; Molinet, p. 409; ODNB under Rhys ap Thomas. Richard's cutting down of William Brandon was greatly to the dismay of one Everard Newchurch, who had lent Brandon 'twelve pounds sterling' to 'go to do your good grace service beyond the sea' and was never paid back; Condon, 'The Kaleidoscope of Treason: Fragments from the Bosworth Story', p. 211.

30. Sandford was perhaps a name for the ford where the stream crossed Fenn Lane. For previous references, see above, pp. xv, 110, 111.

31. Cavill, pp. 35–6; Rolls of Parliament, vol. 6, p. 328; Harl. 433, vol. 3, p. 130; IPM, vol. 1, no. 13.

32. Molinet, p. 408; Goodman and Mackay, p. 96.

33. PV, p. 225. Professor Anne Curry (Bosworth conference, 20 February 2010) suggested that the figure of two hours was because Vegetius, much revered as a source on battle strategy, says that major battles usually took about two hours. In this case it seems unlikely that it would have taken longer.

34. Parry, pp. 3–5; Foss, pp. 39–40, 74–5; Harris, 'The Bosworth Commemoration at Dadlington', pp. 115–31; Nichols, vol. 4, part 2, p. 557. Nichols describes other finds but they all seem to have disappeared. In the case of the one referenced here they may not have been fifteenth-century weapons. It is difficult to see why weapons would not have been looted anyway. Perhaps these had been looted and hidden for future recovery, which might explain why they were so far from the battlefield. Thanks are due to Tom Welsh for this reference.

35. Andre, p. 34, with thanks to Lesley Boatwright for translating the Latin.

36. PV, p. 226; CC, p. 183. There is some evidence that the tradition of where the 'coronation' took place may be correct; the hill and field were called Garbrodys and Garbrod Field in the late fifteenth century but were known as Crown Hill and Crown Field from 1605. The name change in the intervening 120 years may reflect either the truth of the tradition or the legend that had grown up in that time. See Foard, p. 30. The other two men knighted on the battlefield were John Mortimer and Robert Poyntz, Gairdner, pp. 364–5. For plunder, see Bennett, p. 121.

37. Hall's Chronicle says Blanc Sanglier, but the Great Chronicle of London has a 'Pursuivant called Norroy'. John More was Norroy King of Arms in the reign of Richard III so it may have been him or his son, known to have been Blanc Sanglier, who carried his master's body. See Walter Godfrey (ed.), *The College of Arms, Survey of London* (1963), p. 238.
38. PV, p. 226; CC, p. 183; Rous (Hanham), pp. 123–4; Edwards, pp. 29–30; Baldwin, 'King Richard's Grave in Leicester', pp. 21–4. Baldwin sets out the later history of the tomb.

After the Battle

1. Griffiths and Thomas, p. 71.
2. See comments by Chrimes, *Henry VII*, p. 68.
3. Boatwright, Lesley et al., vol. 2, pp. 13–14.
4. CC, p. 183.
5. YHB, vol. 1, pp. 368–9. The Latin phrase should read *vacat regalis pars*. Thanks are due to Lesley Boatwright for this information.
6. YHB, vol. 2, pp. 734–6.
7. Campbell, vol. 1, pp. 36, 86, 437.
8. Cavell, p. 24.
9. PV (Hay), p. 3.
10. Fabyan, p. 673; Great Chronicle, p. 239; PV (Hay), p. 5; Harris, 'Tudor Heraldry at Bosworth', pp. 123–33. Harris discusses whether or not these flags were banners or standards, the sources differ. Henry VIII also used a dun cow as a badge. This actually represented Guy of Warwick, from whom the Beauforts claimed descent through the Beauchamps of Holt; Siddons, vol. 2, part 1, p. 88.
11. Campbell, vol. 1, pp. 178–83.
12. Anglo, pp. 4, 11.
13. Chrimes, *Henry VII*, pp. 62–3.
14. Bennett, pp. 129, 130; CC, p. 195; Rolls of Parliament, vol. 6, pp. 275–8; Plumpton Correspondence, pp. 48–9. See Appendix 3.
15. Campbell, vol. 1, pp. 579–81; Bennett, p. 130.
16. Cavell, pp. 26–7, 70–82; YHB, vol. 2, pp. 79, 81–5.
17. PV (Hay), p. 11.
18. For a brief account of the battle of Stoke and the events leading up to it, see Goodman, pp. 99–106. See also Cavell, pp. 29–33, 111–20 for an eye-witness account of the battle.

Appendix I
1. See comments by Goodman and Mackay, p. 193.
2. See the analysis of Vergil's work in Ross, pp. xxii–xxvi.
3. See the discussion on authorship by Pronay and Cox, *Crowland Chronicle Continuations 1459–1486*, pp. 78–98.
4. Ross, pp. xliv–xlv.
5. Ross, pp. 235–7. See the annotated list of names in Colin Richmond, pp. 237–42.
6. Bennett, p. 11; LB, p. 363; The Rose of England, p. 194.
7. See the discussion of Mancini's work in Ross, pp. xli–xliii.

Appendix II
1. Reprinted from Harl. 433, vol. 3, pp. 125–8. Lists of the commissioners for all the counties involved in this commission are in CPR, pp. 488–92.
2. Grummitt, pp. 128–30.

Appendix III
1. Lander, pp. 144–8; Cavill, pp. 36–7.
2. Lander, p. 309.
3. Printed from the Rolls of Parliament, vol. 6, pp. 275–8.

Appendix IV
1. See Goodman and MacKay, pp. 92–5; Hanham, p. 55.
2. Quoted from Hanham, p. 123.
3. From Pronay and Cox, *Crowland Chronicle Continuations*, p. 183.
4. Translated from Molinet, vol. 3, p. 409.
5. Quoted (in a slightly revised form) from Vergil (Ellis), pp. 225, 227.
6. The unnamed knight is called Sir William Harrington in the Song of Lady Bessy (pp. 360–1). Sir William is not otherwise known to have been present. The quotation is from the Ballad of Bosworth Field; Hales and Furnival, vol. 3, pp. 256–7. The Song of Lady Bessy is almost identical to this.
7. PV, p. 226.
8. Siddons, vol. 2, part 1, pp. 148–50.
9. Curry, p. 221.
10. Jones, pp. 22, 159–60.
11. CC, p. 183.
12. Edward Hawkins, *Medallic Illustrations of the History of Great Britain and Ireland to the death of George II*, ed. A.W. Franks and H.A. Grueber, vol. 1 (1885), pp. 19–20.

Appendix V
1. Lesley Boatwright, *Ricardian Bulletin* (December 2011), pp. 28–9; John Alban, 'The Will of a Norfolk Soldier at Bosworth', *The Ricardian*, vol. 22 (2012), pp. 1–7.

Appendix VI
1. Richard Buckley, Matthew Morris, Jo Appleby, Turi King, Deidre O'Sullivan and Lin Foxhall, "The king in the car park': new light on the death and burial of Richard III in the Grey Friars church, Leicester, in 1485', *Antiquity*, vol. 87 (2013), pp. 519–38.
2. Rous (Hanham), pp. 123–4.
3. Buckley *et al.*, *op. cit*, p. 535.
4. Rous (Hanham), pp. 121, 123. Rous is the only contemporary chronicler to describe correctly Richard's uneven shoulders.
5. A. Rai, 'Richard III: the final act', *British Dental Journal*, vol. 214, no. 6 (2013), p. 416.
6. Buckley *et al.*, p. 536; Matthew Symonds and Carly Hilts, 'Reconstructing Richard III: Discovering the man behind the myth', *Current Archaeology*, vol. 24, no. 277 (2013), p. 18.
7. With many thanks to Dr Toby Capwell, Curator of Arms and Armour at the Wallace Collection, for discussing with me cavalry charges, the helmet that Richard might have worn and how it could (or could not) have been removed.
8. With many thanks to Bob Woosnam-Savage, Curator of European Edged Weapons at the Royal Armouries, for discussing with me the question of the weapons used to kill Richard.
9. Symonds and Hilts, pp. 14–15; Buckley *et al.*, *op. cit.*, p. 536.
10. Lynda Pidgeon, 'Who killed Richard III?', *Ricardian Bulletin* (December 2012), pp. 48–9; Salon, Society of Antiquaries of London online newsletter, issue 294, 4 March 2013, Feedback.

Bibliography

Acts of Court of the Mercers Company, 1453–1527, ed. Letitia Lyell (1936)

Andre, Bernard, *Life of Henry VII*, ed. James Gairdner (Rolls Series, 1858)

Anglo, Sydney, 'The Foundations of the Tudor dynasty: the Coronation and Marriage of Henry VII', in *The Guildhall Miscellany*, vol. 2 (1960)

Antonovics, A.V., 'Henry VII, King of England, By the Grace of Charles VIII, King of France', in *Kings and Nobles in the Later Middle Ages* (1986)

Armstrong, C.A.J., 'Distribution and Speed of News etc, in England, France and Burgundy', in *England, France and Burgundy in the Fifteenth Century* (1983)

Arthurson, Ian, and Kingwell, Nicholas, 'The Proclamation of Henry Tudor as King of England, 3 November 1483', in *Historical Research*, vol. 63 (1990)

Ashdown-Hill, John, 'The Bosworth Crucifix', in *Transactions of the Leicestershire Archaeological. and History Society*, vol. 78 (2004)

Attreed, Lorraine C. (ed.), *York House Books, 1461–1490*, 2 vols (1991)

Baldwin, David, 'King Richard's Grave in Leicester', in *Transactions of the Leicestershire Archaeological and Historical Society*, vol. 60 (1986)

'Ballad of Bosworth Field', in *Bishop Percy's Folio Manuscript*, ed. J.W. Hales and F.J. Furnivall, vol. 3 (1868)

Barnard, Francis, *Edward IV's French Expedition of 1475* (1925)

Bennett, Michael, *The Battle of Bosworth* (1985)

Boatwright, Lesley, 'The Buckinghamshire Six at Bosworth', *The Ricardian*, vol. 13 (2003)

Boatwright, Lesley, Habberjam, Moira and Hammond, Peter (eds), *The Logge Register of Prerogative Court of Canterbury Wills 1479–1486* (2008)

Buck, George, *History of King Richard the Third*, ed. A.N. Kincaid (1979)

Calendar of Charter Rolls, vol. 6 (1927)

Calendar of Close Rolls, 1476–1485 (1961)

Calendar of Inquisitions Post Mortem and other analogous documents, Henry VII, 3 vols (1898, 1915, 1955)

Calendar of Patent Rolls, 1476–1485 (1954)

Campbell, William (ed.), *Materials for a History of the Reign of Henry VII*, 2 vols (Rolls Series, 1873, 1877)

Cavell, Emma, *The Herald's Memoir 1486–1490* (2009)

Cavill, P.R., *The English Parliaments of Henry VII, 1485–1504* (2009)

Chrimes, S.B., 'The Landing Place of Henry of Richmond, 1485', in *Welsh History Review*, vol. 2 (1964)

——, *Henry VII* (1972)

Commynes, Philippe de, *Memoirs, The Reign of Louis XI, 1461–1483*, transl. Michael Jones (1972)

Complete Peerage of England, Scotland, Ireland and the United kingdom, ed. Vicary Gibbs et al, 14 volumes (1910–1995)

Condon, Margaret, 'The Kaleidoscope of Treason: Fragments from the Bosworth Story', in *The Ricardian*, vol. 7, no. 92 (1986)

——, '22 August 1485: the Battle of Bosworth', the record of an exhibition mounted at the Public Record Office to mark the quincentenary of the battle of Bosworth (1986)

Contamine, Philippe de, *War in the Middle Ages*, transl. Michael Jones (1984)

Conway, A.E., *Henry VII's Relations with Scotland, 1485–98* (1932)

Coote, Lesley and Thornton, Tim, 'Richard, Son of Richard: Richard III and Political Prophecy', in *Historical Research*, vol. 73 (2000)

Coventry Leet Book or Mayor's Register, ed. Mary Dormer Harris (Early English Text Society, OS 135, part 2, 1908)

Crowland Chronicle Continuations, 1459–1486, ed. Nicholas Pronay and John Cox (1986)

Curry, Anne, *Agincourt, a New History* (2005)

Dillon, H.A., 'On a MS. collection of ordinances of chivalry of the 15th century belonging to Lord Hastings', in *Archaeologia*, vol. 57 (1900)

Dobson, R.B., 'Richard III and the Church of York', in *Kings and Nobles in the Later Middle Ages; a Tribute to Charles Ross* (1986)

Edwards, Rhoda, 'King Richard's Tomb at Leicester', in *Richard III: Crown and People*, ed. J. Petre (1985)

——, *The Itinerary of King Richard III, 1483–1485* (1983)

Fabyan, Robert, *New Chronicles of England and of France*, ed. Henry Ellis (1811)

Firth, C.H., 'The Ballad History of the Reigns of Henry VII and Henry VIII', in *Transactions of the Royal Historical Society*, 3rd series, vol. 2 (1908)

Foard, Glenn, 'Bosworth Uncovered', *BBC History Magazine*, vol. 11, no. 3 (2010)

Foss, Peter, *The Field of Redemore: The Battle of Bosworth, 1485* (2nd edn, 1990)

Gairdner, James, *History of the Life and Reign of Richard the Third* (1898)

Goodman, Anthony, and Mackay, Angus, 'A Castilian Report on English Affairs', *EHR*, vol. 88 (1973)

——, *Wars of the Roses: Military Activity and English Society 1452–97* (1981)

Grant, Alexander, 'Foreign Affairs under Richard III', in *Richard III, A Medieval Kingship*, ed. John Gillingham (1993)

Gravett, Christopher, *Bosworth 1485* (1999)

The Great Chronicle of London, ed. A.H. Thomas and I.D. Thornley (1938)

Green, R. Firth, 'Historical notes of a London citizen, 1483–1488', *EHR*, vol. 96 (1981)

Griffiths, R.A., *The Principality of Wales in the Middle Ages; The Structure and Personnel of Government. Part 1, South Wales, 1277–1536* (1972)

——, 'Henry Tudor, the training of a king', in *Huntingdon Library Quarterly* (1986)

—— and Thomas, Roger, *The Making of the Tudor Dynasty* (1985)

Grummitt, David, 'War and Society in the North of England', *Northern History*, vol. 45 (2008)

Hairsine, R.C. and P.B., 'The Chancellor's File, Part 1', in *The Ricardian*, vol. 5 (1979)

Hall, Edward, *Hall's Chronicle; Containing The History of England During the Reign of Henry IV and the Succeeding Monarchs*, ed. Henry Ellis (1809)

Hammond, P.W. and Sutton, Anne F., *Richard III: The Road to Bosworth Field* (1985)

Hampton, W.E., 'John Nesfield', in *Richard III: Crown and People*, ed. J. Petre (1985)

Hanham, Alison, *Richard III and his Early Historians 1483–1535* (1975)

Harris, O.D., 'The Bosworth Commemoration at Dadlington', *The Ricardian*, vol. 7 (1985–87)

——, 'The Transmission of the News of the Tudor Landing', *The Ricardian*, vol. 4 (1976–78)

——, 'Tudor Heraldry at Bosworth', *The Ricardian*, vol. 5 (1979–81)

Harrison, Frederick, *Life in a Medieval College: the Story of the Vicars Choral of York Minster* (1952)

Holinshed, Raphael, *The Chronicles of England, Scotlande and Irelande*, 2nd edn (1587)

Holland, P., 'The Lincolnshire Rebellion of March 1470', *EHR*, vol. 103 (1988)

Horrox, Rosemary, *Richard III: A Study in Service* (1989)

—— and Hammond, P.W. (eds), *British Library Harleian Manuscript 433*, 4 vols (1979–1983)

Household Books of John Howard, Duke of Norfolk, 1462–1471, 1481–1483, Intro. Ann Crawford (1992)

Jones, Michael K., *Bosworth 1485: Psychology of a Battle* (2002)

Kendall, Paul Murray, *Richard the Third* (1955)

Lander, J.R., *Crown and Nobility, 1450–1509* (1976)

Letters and Papers Illustrative of the Reigns of Richard III and Henry VII, ed. J. Gairdner (Rolls Series, 1861)

Mancini, Dominic, *The Usurpation of Richard III*, ed. C.A.J. Armstrong (1969)

Molinet, Jean, *Chroniques*, ed. J.A. Buchon (1828)

'The Most Pleasant Song of the Lady Bessy', in *Bishop Percy's Folio Manuscript, Ballads and Romances*, ed. J.W. Hales and F.J. Furnivall, vol. 3 (1868)

Nichols, John, *History and Antiquities of the County of Leicester*, 4 vols (1795–1815)

Nokes, Elizabeth and Wheeler, Geoffrey, 'Spanish Account etc', in *The Ricardian*, vol. 2, no. 36 (1972)

Owen, Hugh and Blakeway, J.B. *History of Shrewsbury*, vol. 2 (1825)

Palliser, David, 'Richard III and York', in *Richard III and the North*, ed. Rosemary Horrox (1988)

Parry, Timothy, *A Church for Bosworth Field* (1985)

Paston Letters, 1422–1509. Vol. 3, *Edward IV, Henry VII, 1471–1509*, ed. James Gairdner (1875)

Petre, J. (ed.), *Richard III: Crown and People* (1985)

Plumpton Correspondence, ed. Thomas Stapleton (Camden Society, 1839)

Ramsay, James, *Lancaster and York, A Century of British History, AD 1399–1485*, vol. 2 (1892)

Richmond, Colin, '1485 and all that', in *Richard III: Loyalty, Lordship and Law*, ed. P.W. Hammond (2000)

Rolls of Parliament, ed. John Strachey et al, vol. 6 (1777)

'The Rose of England', in *Bishop Percy's Folio Manuscript, Ballads and Romances*, ed. J.W. Hales and F.J. Furnivall, vol. 3 (1868)

Roskell, 'Office and Dignity of the Protector of England', *EHR*, vol. 68 (1953)

Ross, Charles, *Richard III* (1981)

Rous, John, *Rous Roll* (repr. 1980)

——, 'Historia Johannis Rossi Waricensis de Regibus Anglie', in Alison Hanham, *Richard III and his Early Historians* (1975)

Rymer, Thomas (ed.), *Foedera, Conventiones, Literae … et Acta Publica*, Vol. 12, *1475–1502* (1711)

Scofield, C.L., 'The Early Life of John de Vere, 13th Earl of Oxford', *EHR*, vol. 29, no. 114 (1914)

Siddons, Michael, *Heraldic Badges in England and Wales*. Vol. 2, part 1, *Royal Badges* (2009)

Spont, Alfred, 'La Marine Francaise sous la Regne Charles VIII', *Revue des Questions Historiques*, vol. 11 (1894)

Stonor Letters and Papers, 1290–1483, ed. C.L. Kingsford, 2 vols (Camden Society, 1919)

Sutton, Anne F., 'The death of Queen Anne Neville', in *Richard III; Crown and People*, ed. J. Petre (1985)

Sutton, Anne F. and Hammond, P.W. (eds), *The Coronation of Richard III: the Extant Documents* (1983)

Thornton, Tim, 'The Battle of Sandeford: Henry Tudor's understanding of the meaning of Bosworth Field', in *Historical Research*, vol. 78 (2009)

Vale, Malcolm, *War and Chivalry* (1981)

Vergil, Polydore, *Three Books of Polydore Vergil's English History, Comprising the Reigns of Henry VI, Edward IV and Richard III*, ed. Henry Ellis (Camden Society, 1844)

——, *The Anglica Historia of Polydore Vergil, AD 1485–1537*, ed. Denys Hay (Camden Society, 1950)

Warnicke, Retha, 'Lord Morley's statement about Richard III', *Albion*, vol. 15 (1983)

——, 'Sir Ralph Bygod: a Loyal Servant to King Richard III', *The Ricardian*, vol. 6 (1982–84)

Williams, Barrie, 'The Portuguese Connection and the Significance of the Holy Princess', and 'The Portuguese Marriage Negotiations: a Reply', *The Ricardian*, vol. 6 (1982–84)

Williams, Daniel, 'A place mete for twoo battayles to encountre: the siting of the Battle of Bosworth', *The Ricardian*, vol. 7 (1985–87)

Williams, W. Tom., 'Henry of Richmond's Itinerary to Bosworth', *Y Cymmrodor*, vol. 29 (1914)

Wood, Charles, 'Richard III, William Lord Hastings and Friday the Thirteenth', in *Kings and Nobles in the Later Middle Ages*, ed. Ralph Griffiths and James Sherborne (1986)

Index

Note: All peers are indexed under their family names, with a cross reference from the title. Royal peers are indexed under their Christian name with a cross reference, and monarchs, rulers and consorts are indexed under their Christian names.

MMOND P W
ard the III and the Boswor
999/00009 - 1 of 3